UAE
underwater
62 Spectacular Dives

AL MASAOOD mares® just add water

Passionately Publishing...

EXPLORER

UAE Underwater Explorer 2006/3rd Edition
First Published 2001
2nd (Revised) Edition 2002
ISBN 10 976-8182-65-2
ISBN 13 978-976-8182-65-4

Explorer Publishing & Distribution
PO Box 34275, Zomorrodah Building, Za'abeel Road,
Dubai , United Arab Emirates
Phone   (+971 4) 335 3520
Fax   (+971 4) 335 3529
Email   Info@Explorer-Publishing.com
Web   www.Explorer-Publishing.com

Welcome

£2-50 u

Congratulations – you hold in your hands the best dive buddy yet! It's smart, good-looking, wise beyond its years and while it doesn't wear neoprene, it'll never leave wet gear to create a stink in your dive bag either.

This book blends decades of local diving experience thanks to authors Carole Harris and Tony Schroder as well as many underwater enthusiasts in the UAE who have happily offered their knowledge and insight. This means that you benefit from invaluable local dive knowledge that would have taken years to discover otherwise. Together with the publishing and design skills of the Explorer team, this makes the third edition of the **UAE Underwater Explorer** a practical, informative and attractive piece of work.

This third edition also sports a fresh new look, making it easier to use. Some of the dives from our last edition have been affected by the offshore construction taking place and we have either had to remove them, or cover them in brief. However, don't feel hard done by, as we've also added a total of 10 new sites — including the very newest wreck on the west coast, the *Mariam Express*.

All the photography in the guide has been done locally, and all the underwater images are Carole's. The drawings, maps and GPS coordinates have been provided by Tony.

As well as detailing some of the best dives the region has to offer, we've also added an expanded Further Information section with details on the activities that go hand in hand with diving such as snorkelling and dhow or yacht charters; essential first aid knowledge; the lowdown on all aspects of diving and a directory of dive operators and accommodation options to assist you in planning your next dive trip.

While we urge you to get out there and enjoy the diving, just remember that it can be a long journey back to shore and a recompression chamber, so do take care. And, as you explore the reefs and wrecks of this incredible coastline we trust that you'll dive responsibly and with respect for the fragile marine environment.

If you have any comments about the book, or any pearls of diving information, we would be very happy to hear from you. Log on to www.Explorer-Publishing.com and fill in our reader response form – you might even receive another Explorer book for free!

So well done on an excellent acquisition. And here's to fine diving in the UAE and Musandam's most spectacular sites.

The Explorer Team

A big thank you to Al Masaood, with particular thanks to Suresh Balakrishnan, for their sponsorship, and also to Ibrahim N Al-Zu'bi at Emirates Diving Association.

EDA is the non-profit umbrella organization of all dive centers, dive retailers, dive clubs, dive instructors and certified divers in the UAE.

EDA was initiated in 1995 by the instructions of H.H Sheikh Zayed Bin Sultan Al Nahyan, late President of the United Arab Emirates, who felt the importance of diving and the need to protect U.A.E. marine life from further destruction and pollution.

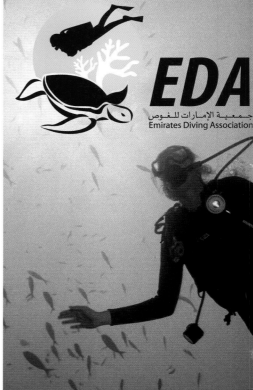

EDA
جـمـعـيـة الإمـارات للـغـوص
Emirates Diving Association

WHAT YOU CAN DO TO HELP!

Become an EDA Member and help EDA in its mission to conserve, protect and restore the U.A.E. marine resources by understanding and promoting the marine environment and promote environmental diving. Join in on our regular activities:

- *Reef Monitoring Project*
- *Clean Up Arabia*
- *Pearl Dive Trips*
- *School Campaigns*
- *Dive For a Cause*

To find out how to become an EDA member, please contact:

EMIRATES DIVING ASSOCIATION
Heritage & Diving Village
Shindaga Area
P.O. Box 33220
Dubai, UAE

Tel:**+971-4-3939390**   Fax: **+971-4-3939391**
Email: **edadiver@emirates.net.ae**

www.emiratesdiving.com

U.A.E. When all you want to do is get wet...
East Coast Diving Resort

open seven days a week, operating three dives daily:

09:30h   12:00h   15:00h

night dives

full range of PADI courses

Instructor Development

MARES Diving Centre

dive retail shop offering great prices

full equipment rental

underwater cameras, camcorders &
diver propulsion vehicles for rent

swimming pool and classroom on site

fleet of purpose built diving boats

Divers Down, Khorfakkan Diving Centre, P. O. Box 10472,
Khorfakkan/ Sharjah, United Arab Emirates
+971 (0) 9 - 2 37 02 99
email: diversdown@emirates.net.ae
http://www.diversdown.ae

PADI 5 Star Gold Palm IDC Centre S-32339 and Official Project AWARE Partner

Member of

EDA

PROJECT
AWARE
FOUNDATION

OFFICIAL
PARTNER
www.projectaware.org

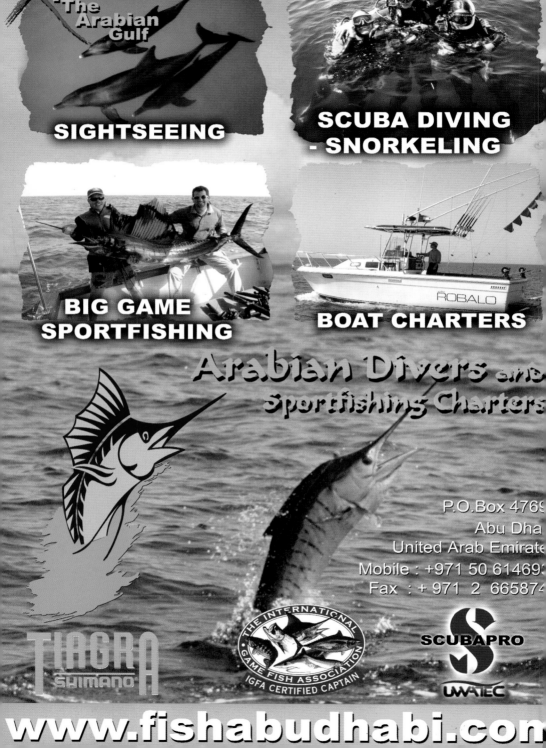

Experience diving with the best.

What your 4WD was made for!

With adventurous routes through the awe-inspiring mountains, wadis and deserts of Oman and the UAE, these off-road guides feature detailed maps, step-by-step directions, stunning photos and everything there is to do and see along the way.

Pick up an Off-Road Explorer today, and remind yourself why you bought a 4WD.

Underwater Explorer

The Authors

Carole Harris

Originally from the coastal town of Portsmouth in the UK, Carole had always dreamt of diving, but the cold UK waters were not particularly appealing. Shortly after arriving in the UAE, she signed up with the BSAC 406 club in Sharjah and completed her first dive course in 1986. She obtained BSAC Advanced Instructor and PADI Dive Master qualifications shortly thereafter.

Her passion with photography extends to the underwater world. Currently she uses a Nikon D70 in a subal housing with a variety of lenses. Carole and her husband have discovered several new species of nudibranchs and she has had numerous photos published in scientific journals. Her images have also appeared in a variety of specialist books, magazines and calendars.

Carole has been resident in the UAE for over 20 years now, has completed more than 3,000 dives and can be found under the water more often than not. See more of her work above and below the waves at www.carole-underwater.com

Tanks and Best Fishes

We would like to thank the following companies and their employees, and all our fellow explorers and dive buddies, for their invaluable input, time, expertise and knowledge – without them we would not have been able to write this book:

- Ali Fikree and Bill Leeman for the drawing of *Ines* and guidance on some of the technical jargon
- Brian Davies for the photographs of the *Energy Determination* and *MV Dara* and for details of the Landing Craft in Khasab
- British Sub Aqua Club 1339/Desert Sports Diving Club for their support and contributions to much of the initial exploration of the region and assistance in compiling info on the dive sites

- Christine Schroder for her steadfast support and all her work in proofreading the book
- Eric Laing and Capt. Joe Finch at Inchcape Shipping Services for donating the Inchcape wrecks and providing all the details
- Guy Ploegaerts who shared in the thrill of being the first to dive on many of the wrecks
- John Gregory for his help with the section on ship weights and measures, and the drawing of the *Neptune* 6
- John Tilley for his assistance in the search for new wrecks
- Kurt Luedi of Maku Dive Center for his ongoing efforts to conserve the reef at Dibba Island

Tony Schroder

Born in Argentina, Tony grew up mainly in England. It was probably the five years he spend with his family stationed in the former colony of Malaya that sparked his great interest in nature. His love of the sea has also been a life-long affair and snorkelling gear is an absolute essential on every trip he takes.

His first experience of diving was with the Jebel Ali BSAC 916 club in 1988. He is now a BSAC First Class Diver and Advanced Instructor with the BSAC 1339 club. As long ago as 1990, Tony started collecting information on wreck sites. The purchase of a GPS in 1991 opened up even more possibilities for locating wrecks and dive sites. He lived in Dubai for over 20 years with his wife Christine, and currently resides in New Zealand.

Tony is an explorer at heart and when he's not investigating submerged wrecks, he enjoys off-road driving. He would love all divers to share in the pleasure this pursuit has given him.

- Leon Betts for keeping an eye on Carole's safety and no-stop limits as she gets carried away with the camera and her subjects. And also for his drawings of various dive sites.
- Maps Geosystems for the satellite images
- Paul Algate at Scuba International for providing further information about Murbah Reef, *Inchcape 10*, Refinery and Deep Reef on the east coast
- Paul Sant at Divers Down for his sketch of the Hole in the Wall
- Phil Holt, dive buddy and invaluable camera holder/protector.
- Phil O'Shea at Pavillon Dive Centre for his assistance with clarifing 'lost wrecks' and details on the *Mariam Express*.
- Seraj Alali at White Sea Shipping for the photographs of the Anchor Barge and the story of her sinking
- Stephanie Davies at Scuba Dubai for her unstinting assistance, constant updates, guidance on equipment and suggestions.
- Stevie Macleod at Scuba Dubai for much needed assistance with technical jargon, and details of Landing Craft in Khasab.
- Stuart Scott Ely for his sketch of Turtle Barge
- Terry Day for a number of photographs of the *Energy Determination*.

IRAN

UAE Dive Sites

ARABIAN GULF

KHASAB
MUSANDAM
(SULTANATE OF OMAN)

DIBBA

UMM AL QUWAIN

AJMAN

SHARJAH

DUBAI

OMAN
UAE

FUJAIRAH

UAE

ABU DHABI

SULTANATE
OF OMAN

N

0   Scale 1:850,000   100km

These maps are not an authority on international boundaries
© Explorer Group Ltd. 2006

Diving in the UAE

The UAE offers diving that's really very special; the lower Arabian Gulf and the Gulf of Oman will satisfy all tastes and levels of experience for divers and snorkellers alike. You can choose from over 30 wrecks in relatively shallow water, tropical coral reefs and dramatic coastlines that are virtually undived. And these are bathed in warm water all year round.

Water temperatures range from a cooler 20°C in January to a warmer 35°C in July and August. Although the land temperatures can be in the high 40's in the summer months, it is rarely too hot when out at sea or dipping into the water. Rain usually falls in the early months of the year, January – March, but it is infrequent and never lasts for long.

elsewhere in the UAE, offering only a sprinkling of hotels and holiday resorts. In sharp contrast, the west coast has seen a huge amount of development in the last 25 years, especially in Abu Dhabi and Dubai. Numerous hotels, including plenty of a luxury five-star standard, offer all the facilities a tourist can reasonably expect, and much more.

The weather on the east coast can be very different to that in the west of the country. On the Gulf of Oman it is slightly cooler in the summer and there may occasionally be rain in late July and August. The weather will often be calm on this coast, while the west coast is being buffeted by a 'shamal' (moderate northerly winds). If your

Areas to Dive

For the purposes of this book we've divided the region into three main areas; the West Coast (lower Arabian Gulf), the Musandam, and the East Coast (on the Gulf of Oman and the Indian Ocean side of the peninsula).

Modern highways connect the coasts of the UAE. From the northern emirates, the journey from the west to the east coast is a two-hour drive, passing through rolling sand dunes, gravel plains and oasis towns, before crossing the rugged western Hajar Mountains and down to the palm-covered coastal strip of the east coast. Development here is not as advanced as

dive on one coast is cancelled because of rough seas or high winds, the weather will probably be fine on the other coast.
The Musandam is the area to the north of the UAE at the very tip of the peninsula, and is actually part of the Sultanate of Oman. This mountainous region is very beautiful and virtually undeveloped. Its remoteness and lack of access means it is one of the least explored diving areas in the world.

Only one paved road runs north from Ras Al Khaimah in the UAE, to Khasab, capital of the Musandam, and many of the small fishing villages along the coast are only accessible by boat or off-road tracks. The only hotels are located in Khasab.

Diving

There are many excellent diving centres and clubs operating here that will help you enjoy the region's wonderful diving. For the **UAE Underwater Explorer** we have covered as many dive sites as possible with the aim of giving a good representation of the best known and most popular locations. Since most visitors to the UAE are based in Dubai, we have included a large number of west coast dive sites.

Only a few dive sites are safely accessible from the shore, so plan on using a boat. If you have your own boat, there are many slipways available and we have included maps and GPS co-ordinates of the best ones. There are also several first class marinas where you can permanently moor your boat (for a fee).

Diver Certification

If you are a certified diver, always remember to pack your certification card - without it no dive organisation in the UAE will allow you to dive.

Learning to dive or advancing your existing qualifications with an internationally recognised organisation is very easy to accomplish in the UAE. This can be arranged through one of the many excellent dive centres. Refer to the Dive Directory (p.181) for contact information.

Levels of Experience

The dive sites described in this book are chosen to suit all levels of diving experience. *Energy Determination* and the Musandam are more challenging and require additional precautions to be safely dived. They are recommended only for more experienced divers. *Ines* is for qualified technical divers only. For all the other dive sites described, we advise you to take the usual precautions and assess conditions at the time of your dive.

Take Care

As with all advice, comments, opinions, directions and suggestions, make sure that you first evaluate the information for yourself - use your common sense, know your limits and dive with caution.

We strongly recommend that you have completed the necessary training before attempting a dive. The minimum qualification you should have is that of an open water diver, which allows you to dive to 18m. The advanced courses that allow you to specialise in wreck, navigation or other skills will make more sites available to you and increase your enjoyment of the sport.

Explorer Group Ltd, Explorer Publishing, Al Masaood and Emirates Diving Association (EDA) and their associates accept no responsibility for any accidents, injuries, loss, inconvenience, disasters or damage to persons or property that may occur while you are out and about or using this guidebook. The fact that a site is mentioned does not necessarily mean that it is always diveable or safe.

Ultimately you are responsible for determining your own limitations based on the conditions you encounter.

How to Select a Dive

1) By name

If you know the name of a dive you'd like to look up, head straight for the index on p.188. As many dives also have alternatives to the most commonly used names, we've listed the dives by all known names.

2) By location

The map of UAE Dive Sites (p.xiv) shows all the dives by location in the three areas; west coast, Musandam and east coast.

3) By area

Each of the three individual sections begins with an overview map that shows the location of all the dives featured in that area.

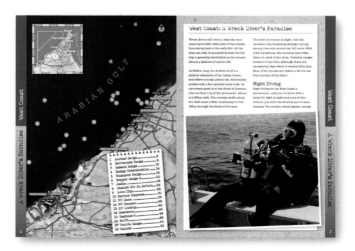

4) By attributes

The Dive Overview Table on p.xxii gives you an at-a-glance look at the attributes of each dive. The depth of the site is listed along with the distance of the site from shore (where multiple harbours have been given we've chosen the harbour closest to the site). Separate columns for different types of dives show whether you can explore a reef or wreck, or if it is a wall or drift dive. There are also columns to show whether you can dive this site at night or snorkel there. In addition, this table lists the dives we believe are the 'must dos' during your time in the UAE.

Dive Overview Table

🥥 Must do

	Dive	Name	Page	Depth (m)	Distance offshore (nm)	Drift	Reef	Wall	Wreck	Snorkelling	Night
W E S T C O A S T	1	Anchor Barge	6	25	18.6				✓		
	2	Barracuda Barge	8	18	4				✓	✓	
	3	Cement Barge	10	12	0.7				✓	✓	✓
	4	Energy Determination 🥥	14	80+	35				✓		
	5	Hammour Barge	18	15	14.9				✓		✓
	6	Hopper Barge 6	20	23	18.7				✓		
	7	Jasim	24	27	28.7				✓		✓
	8	Jazirat Sir Bu Na'air	26	36	43.5	✓	✓			✓	
	9	Lion City	28	30	27				✓		
	10	Mariam Express 🥥	30	21	14.7				✓		
	11	MV Dara	36	20	6.2				✓		
	12	MV Hannan	38	20	33				✓		
	13	MV Ludwig 🥥	40	27	26				✓		
	14	Nasteran	42	23	5.6				✓		
	15	Neptune	44	25	18.7				✓		
	16	Swift	48	38	51.1				✓		
	17	Turtle Barge	50	8	3.1				✓	✓	✓
	18	Zainab 🥥	52	30	18.1				✓		
	19	The Caves	62	10	10.5			✓	✓	✓	✓
	20	Landing Craft	64	10	3.5				✓		
M U S A N D A M	21	Lima Rock 🥥	66	12-60	20.3	✓	✓	✓	✓		
	22	Bu Rashid	69	6-40	–	✓		✓			
	23	Ennerdale Rock	69	16-50	–	✓	✓	✓			
	24	Fanaku Island	70	6-50	–	✓	✓	✓			
	25	Great Quion Island	70	16-50	–	✓	✓	✓			
	26	Hard Rock Cafe 🥥	71	6-20	–	✓	✓	✓			

The Anatomy of a Dive

Each individual site starts with a brief description of the dive, key information about the site, as well as a diagram showing the aspect of the wreck or reef with a north orientation arrow. This means that at a glance you'll be able to see the depth of the dive, any other names it may be known by, GPS coordinates for the location, distances from commonly used harbours for the dive and to or from other sites (for maps of the locations of all harbours, see p.169), and also whether the site is suitable for night dives and snorkelling. Makes dive planning a cinch.

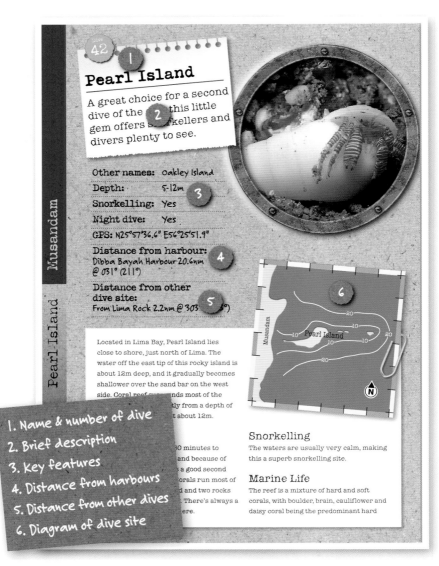

42

Pearl Island

Musandam

Pearl Island

A great choice for a second dive of the ___ this little gem offers s___kellers and divers plenty to see.

Other names: Oakley Island
Depth: 5-12m
Snorkelling: Yes
Night dive: Yes
GPS: N25°57'36.6" E56°25'51.9"

Distance from harbour:
Dibba Bayah Harbour 20.6nm @ 031° (211°)

Distance from other dive site:
From Lima Rock 2.2nm @ 303 ___°)

Located in Lima Bay, Pearl Island lies close to shore, just north of Lima. The water off the east tip of this rocky island is about 12m deep, and it gradually becomes shallower over the sand bar on the west side. Coral reef su___nds most of the ___tly from a depth of ___t about 12m.

___ 30 minutes to ___ and because of ___ a good second ___corals run most of ___d and two rocks ___t. There's always a ___ere.

1. Name & number of dive
2. Brief description
3. Key features
4. Distance from harbours
5. Distance from other dives
6. Diagram of dive site

Pearl Island

Musandam

Snorkelling
The waters are usually very calm, making this a superb snorkelling site.

Marine Life
The reef is a mixture of hard and soft corals, with boulder, brain, cauliflower and daisy coral being the predominant hard

The text for the dive starts with a general introduction to the dive, with either a history of the wreck or a general description of the site and local area. It then goes into detail regarding the Diving, along with specific information on Snorkelling if applicable, and Marine Life.

If the dive is a wreck dive, further details of the vessel can be found on the second page in the Wreck Data info box. This includes type of vessel, size, date sunk and any cargo sunk with the vessel. For more information on wreck data, refer to Shipping Weights and Measures on p.176.

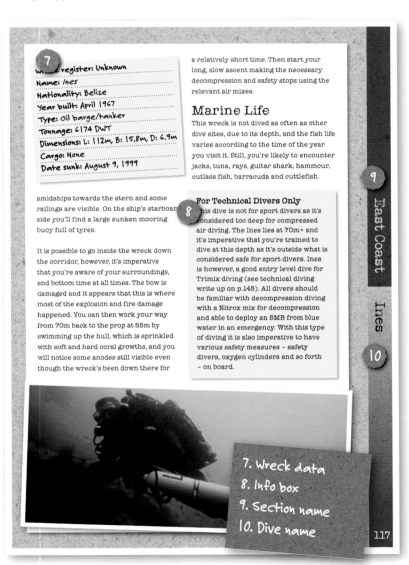

7

Wreck register: Unknown
Name: *Ines*
Nationality: Belize
Year built: April 1967
Type: Oil barge/tanker
Tonnage: 6174 DWT
Dimensions: L: 112m, B: 15.8m, D: 6.9m
Cargo: None
Date sunk: August 9, 1999

a relatively short time. Then start your long, slow ascent making the necessary decompression and safety stops using the relevant air mixes.

Marine Life

This wreck is not dived as often as other dive sites, due to its depth, and the fish life varies according to the time of the year you visit it. Still, you're likely to encounter jacks, tuna, rays, guitar shark, hammour, cutlass fish, barracuda and cuttlefish.

amidships towards the stern and some railings are visible. On the ship's starboard side you'll find a large sunken mooring buoy full of tyres.

8

It is possible to go inside the wreck down the corridor, however, it's imperative that you're aware of your surroundings, and bottom time at all times. The bow is damaged and it appears that this is where most of the explosion and fire damage happened. You can then work your way from 70m back to the prop at 55m by swimming up the hull, which is sprinkled with soft and hard coral growths, and you will notice some anodes still visible even though the wreck's been down there for

For Technical Divers Only
This dive is not for sport divers as it's considered too deep for compressed air diving. The Ines lies at 70m+ and it's imperative that you're trained to dive at this depth as it's outside what is considered safe for sport divers. Ines is however, a good entry level dive for Trimix diving (see technical diving write up on p.145). All divers should be familiar with decompression diving with a Nitrox mix for decompression and able to deploy an SMB from blue water in an emergency. With this type of diving it is also imperative to have various safety measures - safety divers, oxygen cylinders and so forth - on board.

9

East Coast

Ines

10

7. Wreck data
8. Info box
9. Section name
10. Dive name

117

Dive Overview Table

🍂 Must do

	Dive	Name	Page	Depth (m)	Distance offshore (nm)	Drift	Reef	Wall	Wreck	Snorkelling	Night
WEST COAST	1	Anchor Barge	6	25	18.6				✓		
	2	Barracuda Barge	8	18	4				✓	✓	
	3	Cement Barge	10	12	0.7				✓	✓	✓
	4	Energy Determination 🍂	14	80+	35				✓		
	5	Hammour Barge	18	15	14.9				✓		✓
	6	Hopper Barge 6	20	23	18.7				✓		
	7	Jasim	24	27	28.7				✓		✓
	8	Jazirat Sir Bu Na'air	26	36	43.5	✓	✓			✓	
	9	Lion City	28	30	27				✓		
	10	Mariam Express 🍂	30	21	14.7						
	11	MV Dara	36	20	6.2				✓		
	12	MV Hannan	38	20	33				✓		
	13	MV Ludwig 🍂	40	27	26				✓		
	14	Nasteran	42	23	5.6				✓		
	15	Neptune	44	25	18.7				✓		
	16	Swift	48	38	51.1				✓		
	17	Turtle Barge	50	8	3.1				✓	✓	✓
	18	Zainab 🍂	52	30	18.1				✓		
MUSANDAM	19	The Caves	62	10	10.5			✓	✓	✓	✓
	20	Landing Craft	64	10	3.5					✓	
	21	Lima Rock 🍂	66	12-60	20.3	✓	✓	✓		✓	
	22	Bu Rashid	69	6-40	--	✓		✓			
	23	Ennerdale Rock	69	16-50	--	✓	✓	✓			
	24	Fanaku Island	70	6-50	--	✓	✓	✓			
	25	Great Quion Island	70	16-50	--	✓	✓	✓			
	26	Hard Rock Cafe 🍂	71	6-20	--	✓	✓	✓			
	27	Jazirat Al Khayl	71	6-40	--	✓	✓	✓			
	28	Jazirat Hamra	71	6-30	--		✓	✓			
	29	Jazirat Sawda	71	6-30	--		✓	✓			
	30	Jazirat Musandam East Head	72	6-50	--	✓	✓	✓			

	Dive	Name	Page	Depth (m)	Distance offshore (nm)	Drift	Reef	Wall	Wreck	Snorkelling	Night
M U S A N D A M	31	Jazirat Umm Al Fayyarin	72	6-50	--	✓	✓	✓			
	32	Kachalu Island	73	6-40	--	✓	✓	✓			
	33	Ras Dillah	73	6-40	--	✓	✓	✓			
	34	Ras Dillah Ghubbat Ash Shabbus Bay	74	6-30	--		✓	✓			
	35	Ras Khaysah	74	6-25	--	✓	✓	✓			
	36	Ras Musandam	74	6-50	--	✓	✓	✓			
	37	Ras Qabr Al Hindi	75	6-30+	--	✓					
	38	Ras Sarkan	75	6-40+	--	✓		✓			
	39	Ruqq Suwayk	76	6-50+	--	✓	✓	✓			
	40	White Rock	76	6-50+	--	✓	✓	✓			
	41	Octopus Rock	78	5-20	23	✓	✓	✓		✓	
	42	Pearl Island	80	5-12	20.6	✓		✓		✓	
	43	Ras Hamra	82	5-16	18.8	✓	✓	✓		✓	
	44	Ras Lima	84	5-16	18.8	✓	✓	✓		✓	
	45	Ras Marovi	86	6-30	21	✓	✓	✓		✓	
E A S T C O A S T	46	Anemone Gardens	92	20	0.9		✓			✓	✓
	47	Car Cemetery	94	18	1.6				✓	✓	
	48	Coral Gardens	96	26	1.1		✓			✓	✓
	49	Deep Reef	98	30	4.53		✓				
	50	Dibba Island	100	16	12.8		✓			✓	✓
	51	Hole in the Wall	102	15	2.9		✓			✓	✓
	52	Inchcape 1	104	32	7.2				✓		
	53	Inchcape 2	108	22	1.8				✓		
	54	Inchcape 10	114	24	1.53				✓		
	55	Ines	116	72	6.2				✓		✓
	56	Martini Rock	118	3-22	2		✓	✓		✓	
	57	Murbah Reef	120	5-14	8.2		✓			✓	
	58	Ras Qidfa	122	8	2.7		✓	✓		✓	✓
	59	Refinery Reef	124	28	10.8		✓				
	60	Shark Island	126	16	0.8		✓	✓		✓	✓
	61	Sharm Rocks	128	14	5.3		✓	✓		✓	✓
	62	Snoopy Island	130	8	5.5		✓	✓		✓	✓

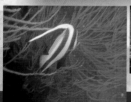

West Coast

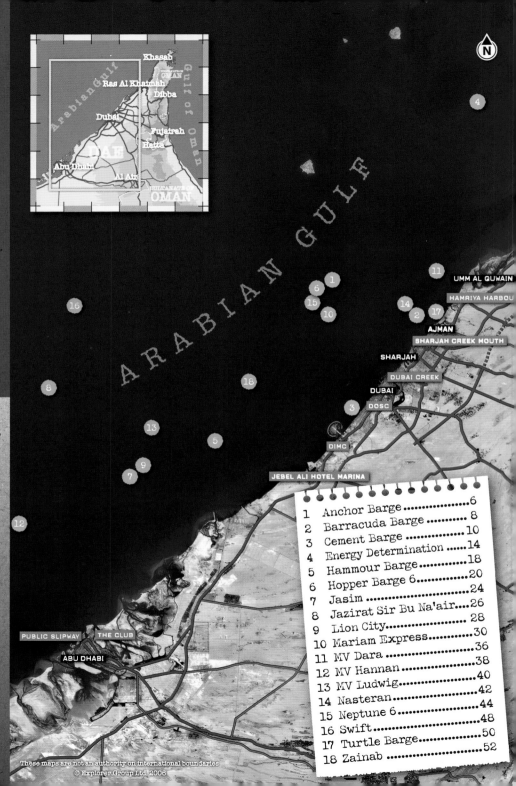

ARABIAN GULF

West Coast: A Wreck Diver's Paradise

Wreck divers will revel in what the west coast has to offer, with some of the wrecks here dating back to the early 60s. All the sites can only be accessed by boat, but the trip is generally worthwhile as the wrecks attract a plethora of marine life.

At 984km long, the Arabian Gulf is a shallow extension of the Indian Ocean, and offers a sandy, almost flat, featureless seabed with a few isolated coral reefs. Its narrowest point is at the Strait of Hormuz (the northern tip of the peninsula), where it is 56km wide. The average depth along the UAE coast is 30m, increasing to over 100m through the Strait of Hormuz.

The tidal movement is slight, with the currents only becoming stronger during spring tides and around the full moon. With a few exceptions, the currents have little effect on most of the dives. Visibility ranges between 5 and 15m, although there are exceptional days when it reaches 20m plus. Most of the wrecks are within a 30 minute boat journey of the shore.

Night Diving

Night diving on the West Coast is spectacular; until you've dived with a powerful light at night and seen all the colours, you won't know what you've been missing. The wrecks, which appear orange

A Wreck Diver's Paradise

and muddy brown during the day, turn into rainbows of colour at night and a whole new set of marine residents appear to feed and forage on and around them.

The wrecks offer such a small area of sanctuary for the fish that they have to hide in every available hole, crevice and corner. As a diver this means that you can get very close to a wide variety of resting fish.

At night, sites like *Nasteran* and Cement Barge are always special and memorable. With the exception of the *Jasim*, *Lion City* and *MV Ludwig*, we have dived all the sites covered in this book at night, even the *Energy Determination*.

A word of caution when returning from the more distant sites, especially at night when everyone wants to get home as quickly as possible. Beware as running into unmarked fishing nets is a very real danger. The nets jam around the propellers, immobilising the boat. There's also sometimes the odd piece of semi-submerged debris drifting about which is difficult to spot, particularly at night, and easily run into.

Diver Safety

To ensure that your wreck dives are safe and enjoyable, keep the following points in mind:

- Wear protective clothing. The wreck's surface may be covered with stinging hydrocorals and protruding pieces of jagged metal.

- Do not enter a wreck without appropriate training.

- If it's your first time on a site and you don't have a dive guide, do not enter the wreck unless a large exit point is visible on the other side.

- Be extra careful if you're diving a wreck after a storm; it may have become unstable or fragile.

- If you intend to penetrate a wreck, take along a rope or guideline that you can tie to the outside of the structure, and use to help you find your way out.

- Take a torch or flashlight.

- Once you swim inside the wreck be cautious, as wrecks tend to silt up quickly. By controlling your finning techniques you'll minimise the chance of stirring the silt up and clouding the visibility.

THINK DEEP.
THINK SHALLOW.
THINK HARD.

GO2 SERIES

STRETCH NEPTUNE 4D- 11+, 20+, 25+, and 30+

BABY 1-Minus ELITE SERIES

HARD NOSE

THINK MANN'S.

For over 50 years, Manns has been thinking up new and better ways to catch fish. We've listened to fishermen's wants and needs, and responded with innovations including:

- the **15+ and 20+ Go2 SERIES** - remarkable lure designed to dive predetermined depths of 15+ and 20+ feet. They feature textured body surfaces, realistic paint finishes, premium hooks, and Mann's exclusive, patented lip design.
- the **BABY 1-MINUS ELITE SERIES** - natural extension of the world-famous Baby 1-Minus, featuring a textured finish with incredibly realistic graphics, louder rattles and premium hooks.

- the **STRETCH NEPTUNE 4D SERIES** - loaded to the gills with all the original performance features that fishermen demanded from the original Stretch, but enhanced to include holographic bodies, dimensional eyes, and extra-strong red hooks.
- and now the all-new **HARDNOSE** series - the first soft bait with a hard head that stays put on the hook. It's the **only** soft plastic bait that needs no special hook, peg, or glue.

One fast-selling, revolutionary idea after anohter.
From the people known for thinking big - and doing the unthinkable.

AL MASAOOD

For more information visit www.masaoodmarine.com or email at marinesports@masaood.com

PO Box 322 Abu Dhabi, UAE
Tel. No. + 971 2 6424222

PO Box 3945 Dubai, UAE
Tel. No. + 971 4 3241544

Mann's BAIT COMPANY™

The Anchor Barge while being sunk

Dive 1

Anchor Barge

A site well worth exploring and a good place to watch the cuttlefish go by.

Depth:	25m
Snorkelling:	No
Night dive:	Yes

GPS: N25°30'47.6" E55°04'35.7"

Distance from harbours:
Abu Dhabi Club 70.6 @ 32° (212°)
DIMC 25.4nm @ 350° (170°)
Dubai Creek 18.6nm @ 319° (139°)

Distance from other dive sites:
HB6 (p.20) 0.6nm @ 59° (239°)
Neptune 6 (p.44) 0.7nm @ 55° (235°)

Sunk by the White Sea Shipping Company in 1998 to form an artificial reef, the anchor barge is a large upside down wreck. She rests on her forward machinery cabin in 23-25m of water, and the roomy open area between her deck and the seabed means that there's plenty of hiding space for sea creatures. The cabin contains the anchor winches and the cargo and ballast transfer pumps, with her bulk being supported by the cabin and deck equipment.

Diving

The wreck lies on a ridge of rock almost a metre high, making this one of the few dive sites in the Gulf where the seabed has some features that are worth exploring. You should take a powerful torch to search under the hull of the barge. Make sure you look up at whatever has taken up residence on the overhead deck.

As the vessel is rectangular and slab-sided and the currents can be quite strong on this site, it can sometimes be rather difficult to anchor here.

Wreck register: Unknown
Name: Pontoon 300 (formerly *The Leena*)
Nationality: Unknown
Year built: Unknown
Type: MV barge
Tonnage: 3,900 tonnes
Dimensions: L: 82m, B: 27m, D: 5m
Cargo: Ballast
Date sunk: April 1998

Marine Life

The marine growth established itself on the wreck with scallops, oysters and small clumps of black sea squirts being the first to take hold, and hydrocorals covering all the surfaces and blurring the edges. On the surrounding sand and rocky bottom, flatworms (black with a colourful orange edging) abound in February and March.

You also have a good chance of seeing cuttlefish on this site. These amazing creatures have a neon-like line that runs around their mantle, and they can alter their colour and shape to blend in with their surroundings.

Going Artificial

The benefit of sinking an old vessel, or even an obsolete rig, is that it provides a habitat for hundreds of underwater species to live and feed on. This is generally a positive change, especially where the seabed is largely flat and featureless. It's no guarantee that a wreck will become a healthy and diverse reef, but the chances are that nature will snap up the opportunity.

To read an account of how a wreck is gradually transformed into a reef, turn to p.111 and read 'A Year in the Life of *Inchcape 2*'.

The Anchor Barge being sunk ↗

Dive 2

Barracuda Barge

This old barge is now home to plenty of barracuda, particularly in the cooler months.

Depth:	18m
Snorkelling:	Yes
Night dive:	No

GPS: N25°27′15.6″ E55°22′41.4″

Distance from harbours:
Ajman Creek 4nm @ 298° (118°)
DIMC 25.1nm @ 30° (210°)
Hamriya Harbour 6.3nm @ 256° (76°)
Sharjah Creek 4.6nm @ 353° (173°)

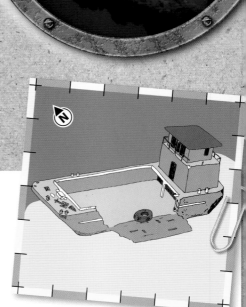

Although the circumstances of loss aren't fully known, the fact that the vessel's engine and steering gear have been removed would suggest that a local fisherman sunk this barge to form an artificial reef. In the winter of 1997, a fisherman told Blue Planet Diving about the wreck and its location.

The barge sits upright in 18m with her bow facing 340°. The seabed is flat and featureless and there are a few bits of wreckage scattered about. Unusually, for a barge, the wheelhouse and engine room are double-storeyed.

Several windows and doors give divers easy access to the interior, but when you enter the small rooms be careful not to stir up the silt, which dramatically reduces the visibility.

The top of the wheelhouse is at 10m and covered in algae and shells. You'll find small shoals of surprisingly tame fish congregating around it.

The small wreck is easily circumnavigated several times in a dive. Take your time inspecting the outside hull and look for small gobies with shrimp in their sandy homes on the seabed. Then explore the hold before you go in and out of the wheelhouse. Check out the unusual anchor still sitting on the bow.

Snorkelling

Snorkellers will enjoy this site and will see the wheelhouse easily from the surface.

Marine Life

During the winter months this wreck is surrounded by shoals of barracuda, although during the summer months they move to cooler, deeper water. Barracuda Barge is also home to the usual yellow snappers. These fish literally engulf the wreck, swimming above, around and within it, and squeezing into every available nook and cranny, no matter how small.

The cowries you'll see here are a similar rusty-brown colour to the ones found on *MV Dara*, which is a result of them absorbing the iron oxide from the rusting barge. The wreck is covered in various types of orange, red, brown and black sponges, and lots of barnacles with their feathery arms that feed on small algae and other morsels. Several types of nudibranchs inhabit this wreck, their gills pulsing as they breathe (look to see if you can find their eggs in circular patterns close by). You'll also notice a white, fern-like plant; take care as these are stinging hydroids and may give you a nasty sting or rash.

Wreck register: Not charted
Name: Original name unknown
Nationality: Unknown
Year built: Unknown
Type: MV coastal barge – single screw
Tonnage: 800 tonnes gross
Dimensions: L: 30m, B: 10m, D: 4m
Cargo: None
Date sunk: Unknown

Barracuda

Cement Barge

A good choice for most types of training dives, with varied marine life from squirts to stingrays.

Depth:	12m
Snorkelling:	Yes
Night dive:	Yes

GPS: N25°10'19.7" E55°12'17.7"

Distance from harbours:
DIMC 5.7nm @ 034° (214°)
DOSC 0.7nm @ 257° (77°)
Dubai Creek 7.8nm @ 217° (37°)

This cement barge sank in 1971 when it ran into heavy weather en route to Dubai. It sits more or less intact and upright in 12m of water, but it has begun to deteriorate, with large cracks and holes appearing along the hull. The barge still carries its original cargo of cement and the bags can be clearly seen. The depth from the surface to the top of the superstructure is approximately 5m, and the average depth of the deck and holds is 8-10m.

Diving

Start your dive on the sandy bottom and swim around the wreck. Look under the stern for the hammour and snapper that like to hide in the depression where the sand has been washed away beneath the propeller shaft. On the port side of the stern lie the remains of the funnel. Make your way forward, taking time to investigate the numerous holes where the hull rests.

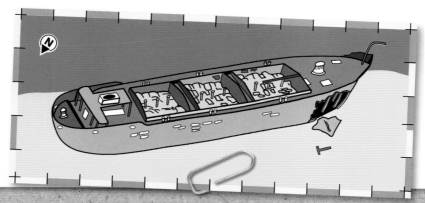

Wreck register: 108300778 &
Lloyds wreck no. 204

Name: Alamina

Nationality: Iraqi

Year built: Unknown

Type: Motor lighter, single screw

Tonnage: Gross tonnage unknown

Dimensions: L: 25m, B: 7m, D: 7m

Cargo: 1,200 tonnes of cement

Date sunk: May 6, 1971

The lower section of the bow has collapsed leaving an opening right through the wreck. All that remains of the bridge and cabin is the framework. The separate holds still contain their cargo of cement bags, but the bulkheads are breaking up; if you use a bright light, you'll often find large fish resting in the gaps. The hatch cover to the engine room is missing and despite the space being silted up, you can still see the remains of the engines.

The Cement Barge is always worth a visit; not only is it an excellent site for most types of training dives, but it also offers some of the best night diving around. A short journey from most of the harbours on the west coast, this reef of cement and metal is a magnet for a variety of fish, night and day.

Snorkelling

One of the few wrecks that's shallow enough to make snorkelling possible, the cement barge is easily viewed from the surface. For those with a good lung capacity, the whole of the top section is worth a duck dive down to explore.

Marine Life

There's always an abundance of fish on this wreck, which has several resident clownfish nestling within the anemones. Sponges, thorny oysters, sea squirts, clams, scallops and barnacles cover every available surface, including the cement bags. The holes and cracks hide a variety of fish, including hammour (although this wreck is well fished, so they tend to be small). Despite being a popular fishing spot, the fish are very tame. On one particular dive, we were 'mobbed' by Arabian angelfish, batfish and sergeant majors.

Gobies and their symbiotic shrimp can be seen in the sand surrounding the hull. The gobies guard the hole while the shrimp busily clear sand from their homes. You'll have to be very patient to see the shrimp though, as they dart back into the safety of their home at any sign of movement.

Blennies hide in small holes, and there are several species of dottybacks, small, beautifully coloured fish that are always nearby in search of a titbit. Large shoals of yellow snapper surround the wreck and sometimes you'll see schools of juvenile barracuda patrolling the perimeter. Keep an eye out for stingrays – difficult to spot as they're usually covered with sand with only their tail visible.

Arabian angelfish

Underwater Abstracts

The fin detail of a scorpionfish

Daisy coral

Parrot-fish skin detail with shrimp

Toxic urchin

Starfish

Pufferfish skin detail

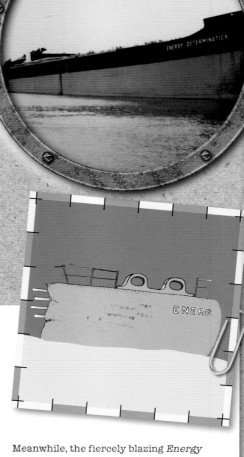

Energy Determination

This wreck has an interesting story behind it and plenty of scope for exploration.

Depth:	80m+
Snorkelling:	No
Night dive:	No

GPS: N26°04'08.1" E55°34'04.1"

Distance from harbours:
DOSC 56.7nm @ 018° (198°)
Dubai Creek 49.9nm @ 016° (196°)
Hamriya Harbour 35nm @ 004° (184°)
Sharjah Creek 42.5nm @ 13° (193°)

The *Energy Determination* sailed with ballast from Bonaire, Netherlands Antilles on November 5, 1979. She was bound for Das Island in the Gulf, where she was due to load a cargo of crude oil. However, at 01:00 local time on December 13, as the *Energy Determination* was passing through the Strait of Hormuz, about 64km from Ras Al Khaimah, there was an enormous explosion. A fire broke out near the number 9 starboard tank, which contained 354 tons of slops. Fire and smoke quickly spread to the engine room and living quarters.

The captain decided to abandon ship and the life rafts were deployed. Of her 38 man crew, 37 were picked up from their life rafts by an Omani naval vessel that was in the area.

Meanwhile, the fiercely blazing *Energy Determination*, visible over 15km away and with burning fuel oil leaking from a hole in her starboard side, began to list and settle by the stern.

Salvage tugs that had raced to the scene noted that the deck and starboard side had a hole some 13m wide from the bridge house towards the bow. The salvage crews managed to get a line on board and they

Wreck register: 10830047
Name: *Energy Determination*
Nationality: Liberian
Year built: Unknown
Type: VLCC (very large crude carrier)
Tonnage: 321,186 DWT, 250,000 tonnes gross
Dimensions: L: 350m, B: 55m, D: 22m
Cargo: Ballast
Date sunk: December 15, 1979

towed the crippled ship to a safe position clear of the shipping lanes.

At 04:30 on December 15, *Energy Determination* broke in two, 27m forward of the bridge superstructure. The stern section containing the engine room, accommodation and pump room sank east of Mina Saqr at a depth of approximately 80m. The bow section was towed towards Dubai and anchored 11km off the coast for over two years, until it was sold to South Korean shipbreakers.

She left Dubai under tow on March 1, 1982. The insurance value of the hull and machinery was US$58 million, making her, up until December 1988, the largest total hull loss ever underwritten by Lloyd's.

Whaleshark and company ↱

Energy on fire!

Diving

Diving the *Energy Determination* is not for the inexperienced or faint-hearted. Great care must be taken in the preparation and planning of this dive. The currents can run at over 5 knots, so you should plan to dive in slack water in neap tides. (Tide tables are generally only available for Port Rashid and Khor Fakkan, so some calculations must be made to determine slack water.) You should plan to arrive at the site early to allow for tidal differences in the locality.

Anchoring onto the wreck can be time consuming — due to the depth and current, the line bellies out, not allowing the anchor to reach the wreck. The preferred method is to use a redundant shot line and not to anchor. For safety, an additional cylinder and regulator should be rigged on the shot line at 10m.

The vessel's stern section rests on her port side in 80-90m of water. The wreck lies on an incline, and the depth from the surface to the top of the wreck is about 25m at the forward starboard section, descending to 60m at the stern.

The accommodation deck and machinery flat (the cabin-like structure over the engine room), are more or less intact, but the bridge is canted and partially torn off.

Marble ray

The deck and tank directly forward of the accommodation area have been ripped out, leaving a big jagged hole that has ladders running down into the darkness. This gaping hole extends forward for about 10m to where the deck and hull remain intact. The remaining 25m of deck and hull come to an abrupt end where the bow section has broken off.

Marine Life

The forward 25m section of the hull is covered in yellow, white and red soft corals, and some lime green whip corals. Strong currents allow these corals to grow and when you swim down, their bright colours glow in the gloom.

The fish are big and tame on this site. Among other creatures, you may see large, rather frightening, but surprisingly tame marble rays, or even a whaleshark. One has been photographed at close quarters on this wreck and a particularly lucky dive group were on the wreck when a whaleshark party of five appeared.

The Ol' Fly & Dive

Combining diving and flying is always a little risky, so you should stop diving at least 24 hours before flying to give your body time to rehydrate and degas.

Long flights should be avoided if possible and if you do drink alcohol during the flight you need to top up on even more water than usual to avoid becoming dehydrated.

Salp chain

Dive 5

Hammour Barge

A small, accessible wreck that has been claimed by hammour as their home.

Depth:	15m
Snorkelling:	No
Night dive:	Yes
GPS:	N25°04'40.5" E54°46'06.5"

Distance from harbours:
Abu Dhabi Club slipway
Abu Dhabi Club 39.7nm @ 31° (211°)
DIMC 20.4nm @ 266° (086°)
DOSC 25.1nm @ 255° (075°)
Jebel Ali Marina 14.9nm @ 290° (110°)

Distance from other dive site:
From MV Ludwig (p.40) 11nm @ 102° (282)

The vessel lies upright in 12-15 metres of water. Her hold contains a cargo of pipes that make a perfect home for hammour – which is how the site obtained its name. The wheelhouse is intact, but all the 'goodies' have been removed.

It's not known precisely when this wreck was sunk, but judging by the marine growth on her, she's been resting on the seabed for at least 20 years.

Diving

This is a relatively small wreck with a few scattered pieces of debris lying on the sand nearby. Our suggested dive plan is to start at the base of the vessel and to swim around it, looking on the sand and in the debris for any interesting marine life. Then carry on to inspect the hull of the barge at the point where it rests on the seabed, as this is where many of its smaller residents hide.

The small cabin is accessible and worth exploring. Make sure you take a look inside

Wreck register: 108301272
Name: Unknown
Nationality: Unknown
Year built: Unknown
Type: Open hold barge
Tonnage: 860 tonnes gross
Dimensions: L: 60m, B: 10m, D: 5m
Cargo: Pipes
Date sunk: Unknown

dottyback, and their less colourful cousins, the Gulf dottyback.

Keep an eye out for the several varieties of blennies to be found here. It's amazing how these colourful fish manage to squeeze into the tiniest of spaces, even trying to hide inside empty barnacle shells! They can be seen waiting near or inside their little holes with just the top of their head sticking out, ready to dart out of sight at the first sign of danger. Arabian angelfish can be seen all over the wreck, picking over the encrustations, and you might also spot some moon wrasse.

the pipes in the hold; you will always find some of the resident hammour hiding there.

Marine Life

The wreck is not often visited by divers, which means that the fish life is reasonably tame. These shallow wrecks are often home to the more brightly coloured reef fish like the orange

Warning

Before attempting to dive any wreck it's strongly recommended that you receive adequate training in diving in an overhead environment.

Hammour

Hopper Barge 6

An easy wreck to navigate, with a number of interesting marine inhabitants to observe.

Bat-fish

Depth:	23m
Snorkelling:	No
Night dive:	Yes

GPS: N25°30'27.9" E55°03'58.6"

Distance from harbours:
DIMC 25.1nm @ 349° (169°)
DOSC 21.5nm @ 336° (156°)
Dubai Creek 18.7nm @ 317° (137°)

Distance from other dive site:
From *Neptune 6* (p.44) 0.18nm @ 223° (43°)

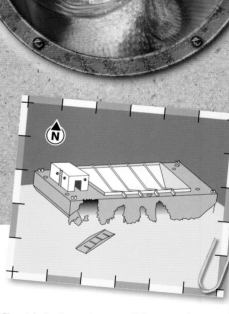

This is another of the wrecks that has been sunk by a local fisherman in close proximity to the *Neptune 6's* marker buoy (see p.44). Under international maritime law, wrecks that could be a hazard to shipping must have a marker buoy, known as a cardinal marker buoy, to indicate where there is clear water to passing vessels. However, the upkeep and maintenance of these buoys is costly (in excess of US$50,000 a year), so fishermen understandably tend to sink vessels near to existing marker buoys, rather than incur the cost of a new buoy.

The HB6 ended up here when she drifted onto the lee breakwater of Port Khalid in Sharjah during a storm on Feburary 18, 1982. The result was a total loss insurance claim. She was later raised, towed to her present location and sunk.

Among the sights here are the barge's drop-bottom doors, which were hydraulically operated, and the two cabins that housed the hydraulic gear on the stern. There's also a large cavity on the starboard side, which is the result of her collision with the breakwater stabits.

Diving

This is an easy wreck for navigation as HB6 sits upright in 25m, with her bows facing south at 180°, and she's situated close to the *Neptune 6*. Her starboard side is beginning to break up and several large holes have exposed the drop-bottom doors. The holes in the side are well worth a visit, and best explored with a torch. Entry into the machinery cabins is also possible.

Marine Life

We once found empty *Cypraea pulchar* cowries here when exploring one of the holes under the wreck. Known locally as 'four-eyes', these beautiful shells are light pinkish brown and have two chocolate brown blotches at each extremity.

Batfish will often follow you nearly all the way to the surface on your ascent. These large fish seem unafraid of divers; the fact that they're not targeted by fishermen could explain their friendliness.

Guitar shark

Wreck register: -
Name: Hopper Barge 6 (HB6)
Nationality: Panamanian registered
Year built: Unknown
Type: Dump barge
Tonnage: 1,000 tonnes gross
Dimensions: L: 48m, B: 14m, D: 5m
Cargo: None
Year sunk: About 1985

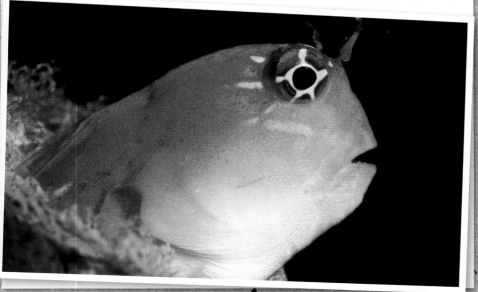

Blenny

Life Under The Palms

The residents of Dubai love a good debate, and nothing fires opinion like discussing the impact of the UAE's offshore construction projects.

What the construction of the UAE's artificial islands (the Palms, The World and the East Coast Island) represents depends on your point of view. To some they're the pinnacle of progress, but to others a supreme folly or an environmental disaster.

Marine experts – and divers – worry that the markedly poor visibility of the coast's waters is the first sign that change is not necessarily for the better. While developers say that the islands will create underwater habitats, others worry about man playing at being Mother Nature.

The Price Of Development

High sea temperatures and increased salinity levels in the late 1990s and early 2000s saw extensive coral bleaching in the region's reefs. While the Environment Agency Abu Dhabi reported in June 2006 that there were indications that Abu Dhabi's reefs are recovering, environmentalists fear that dredging for offshore construction is placing additional pressure on vulnerable reefs. Even beachgoers can see that the coast's once clear waters are now cloudy, and divers and environmentalists have reported finding oyster beds, fields of sea grass and reefs buried and suffocated under deep silt.

Nakheel, the developers of the Palms and The World, say that the disturbance is temporary and that visibility improves within days. They argue that before the islands were built, the seabed consisted mainly of undulating, featureless sand with only a few shipwrecks and the occasional outcrop of limestone to form small reefs. The islands' rocky outer walls, they say, have effectively created hundreds of kilometres of reef.

Artist's impression of The Palm Jebel Ali

Nakheel says that not only have they created new reefs, but that the developments have also given rise to a variety of habitats, including intertidal zones, seagrass meadows, protected estuarine environments and rocky reefs. Their environmental team has recorded sightings of dolphins, manta rays, trevally and sharks within the waters of the Palm Jumeirah (the smallest of the three Palm projects and the closest to being completed at the time of writing).

Marine experts though worry that these artificial reefs aren't a true substitute for the areas that have been destroyed. By changing the marine environment, it's also possible that marine life that wasn't previously seen in the area could move in, challenging native species.

Of immediate concern for many divers is the poor visibility on many sites, rendering them unsuitable for diving. Some losses may be temporary (see the feature 'Dives on Hold' on p.32), but at least two sites have been lost forever.

According to Nakheel, the water quality and visibility is monitored monthly and they report that diving conditions are already 'excellent' in and around the developments. These sites will remain closed to the public though until construction is complete.

A New Place To Dive

To some extent, Nakheel is counting on the diving and snorkelling attractions of the Palms. The Palm Jumeirah is reported to be the site for a planned 'dive park' (apparently complete with gold bars to thrill even the most jaded, been-there, seen-that snorkeller). It's been said that some of the wrecks that made up the Rashid Wrecks site near the old harbour wall have been moved to the Palm, along with two fighter jets and a large aircraft that's been cut up for divers to explore.

But by summer 2006, the only confirmed fact was that the concept was still in the planning phase. Nakheel and the hoteliers on the developments will work together with local dive operators to decide on how they will meet the needs of diving tourists.

As with knowing the true and full impact of the development on the marine environment, it remains a waiting game to see what impact the Palms will have on diving opportunities in the UAE too.

Dive 7

Jasim

It's easy to become completely engrossed in this interesting dive, so keep an eye on your bottom time.

Mottled ray

Depth:	27m
Snorkelling:	No
Night dive:	Yes

GPS: N24°58'47.2" E54°29'43.8"

Distance from harbours:
Abu Dhabi Club 28.7nm @ 12° (192°)
DIMC 36nm @ 258° (78°)
Dubai Creek 46.9nm @ 246° (66°)
Jebel Ali Marina 28.9nm @ 268° (88°)

Once used by the UAE armed forces for target practice, the *Jasim* now rests on her port side, in 26-27m of water. She's broken into three large sections. The stern section consists of the engine room and accommodation, with the large single propeller and rudder still in place. The middle cargo section is a tangled, confused collection of broken hatches, rigging and old vehicle parts and lorry wheels. The bow section is more or less intact with lamp rooms and deck winches.

Diving

This site is always an interesting dive, although care must be taken as the average depth is 27m. Watch your bottom time and allow plenty of air for safety stops. The bridge and living quarters can be accessed through several hatches. The engine room is a little more difficult to enter, although access can be gained through two deck hatches aft of the accommodation area. Once inside, take care not to stir up the deep layer of silt in the engine room.

Wreck register: 108301272

Name: *Jasim*

Nationality: Unknown

Year built: Unknown

Type: MV coastal tanker

Tonnage: 1,200 tonnes gross

Dimensions: L: 60m, B: 10m, D: 5m

Cargo: Ballast

Date sunk: March 25, 1986

Marine Life

This wreck offers the opportunity to see the usual west coast marine life, including several species of brittle stars and cowrie shells. The shells are normally nocturnal, but on this site you can usually find one or two during the day.

There are also many hydrocorals, orange sponges and sea squirts. Although this wreck was sunk 20 years ago, the marine growth is not as advanced as it is on some of the west coast's other wrecks.

The Fog

A foggy mask can really ruin a dive or snorkel trip. Most people have tried any number of things in diving lore, but we have two favourite tricks.

The first is to rub a little toothpaste over the lens. This will get the fine layer of film off the mask (without damaging it) and it smells pretty good too. It's also a good idea to leave a little water in the mask until you put it on as this gets the mask to the same temperature as the sea.

If that doesn't do the job, try a squeeze of Johnson's Baby Shampoo in your mask and then rinse it just before you get into the water. And if you're not too thorough in cleaning the mask off, the beauty of it is. . . no more tears!

Dottyback blenny ↲

Dive
8

Jazirat Sir Bu Na'air

An island sanctuary for magnificent corals, turtles, rays and large pelagic fish.

Manta ray

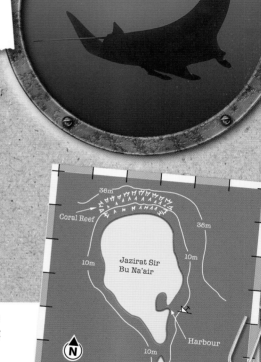

Depth:	36m
Snorkelling:	Yes
Night dive:	Yes

GPS: N25°13'30" E54°13'00"

Distance from harbours:
Abu Dhabi Club 43.5nm @ 348° (168°)
DIMC 51.1nm @ 278° (98°)
Dubai Creek 58.7nm @ 266° (86°)
Jebel Ali Marina 46.3nm
@ 286° (106°)

Jazirat Sir Bu Na'air is an island that lies 70km off the Emirates' coast. Measuring just over 1km long by 0.5 km wide, it's a UAE military outpost and coastguard station, but also a protected turtle breeding area. There are no restrictions on sailing or diving near the island, but it is a sensitive military base so landing is not advisable (although you do occasionally see people picnicking on the beaches).

In 2000, HH Dr Sheikh Sultan bin Mohammed Al Qassimi, Supreme Council Member and Ruler of Sharjah, issued Administrative Order No. 3 that banned all activities considered harmful to the environment of Jazirat Sir Bu Na'air island.

The six article order seeks to halt the deterioration of the island's environment, protect its marine life, and develop its natural resources. This means that fishing all species of turtle, collecting their eggs or damaging their nesting beaches along the island's coastline is strictly prohibited.

The order also bans any activities that could threaten the safety of the island's many resident and migrating bird species.

Diving

This site is characterised by coral reefs, a shelving sandy bottom and lots of drop-offs. Towards the northern end of the island there's a large area of table and staghorn coral in magnificent condition. The coral runs north to the 20m mark and then the seabed shelves down to a depth of more than 30m.

The north-eastern side has large flat rocks and coral, and there are more extensive areas of coral to the north-west. Off the southern tip of the island, the sandy bottom runs to 20m, ending with a small sea mount. At the entrance to the harbour on the south-east side, you'll find the partially submerged wreck of a barge.

Snorkelling

The island isn't just for divers – snorkellers will have a wonderful time here too. The visibility is good, and as it is one of the protected turtle breeding areas, turtles are frequently seen by snorkellers. By using a snorkel, you create less noise and fewer bubbles than divers do, so it's easier to get a closer look at the marine life.

Concentrate on the northern coral field, which starts at 5m and runs gently into deeper water.

Marine Life

The island is rarely visited by divers or fishermen and the resulting lack of disturbance encourages prolific shoals of fish. There are numerous large pelagic fish, spotted eagle rays, barracuda and large rays.

It's a long journey to the island, but the diving and snorkelling at Jazirat Sir Bu Na'air is definitely worth the trip.

The Big Queasy

There are a number of sea sickness tablets you can take – Dramamine, Stugeron and Dezinil – and you may have to try them all out (on different dives, of course) to determine which one suits you best. Some divers wear wrist bands with special pressure points on wrists or patches that look like mini plasters. Called Scopoderm, they are worn behind the ears and can be quite effective. As with all medication, you need to take care of the possible side-effects.

There are also other ways to minimise the chance of feeling seasick. When you're getting ready for a dive try to have all your gear lined up and placed within easy reach. This will enable you to kit up quickly – the last thing you want is to be looking down for any length of time. While you're on the boat try to keep your eyes on the horizon.

If you feel sick after surfacing, you'll feel better if you remove your gear and get back into the water (if it's not rough). Also make sure you drink plenty of fluids to avoid becoming dehydrated.

Green turtle

Shoals of snapper

Dive 9

Lion City

An exercise in orientation and navigation that makes a good second dive.

Depth:	30m
Snorkelling:	No
Night dive:	Yes

GPS: N25°00'13.4" E54°31'43.9"

Distance from harbours:
Abu Dhabi Club 30.4nm @ 14° (194°)
DIMC 33.9nm @ 259° (79°)
DOSC 38.8nm @ 253° (73°)
Jebel Ali Marina 27nm @ 270° (90°)

The *Lion City* – you can still see her name on the bow, and a star emblem on the funnel – lies on her port side in 30m of water with her bow facing 300°. Despite being used for target practice by the UAE military, the vessel is mostly intact with the funnel and some rigging lying on the sand.

The distance from the shore makes this wreck a good second dive if you've been exploring either the *Jasim* (see p.24) or the *MV Ludwig* (see p.40).

Diving

The *Lion City*'s living quarters and engine rooms are easily accessed without much difficulty. If you do want to enter and investigate the interior, remember that the wreck is lying on its side, so keep this in mind when navigating your way around.

Swimming along stairways that don't go up or down and arriving in rooms on their side can be disorientating.

Look at the shape of holes in the wreck and decide which is the easiest way for you to fit through. Don't forget that with your tank and BCD you are now deeper than you are wide. If you feel yourself becoming stuck, reverse immediately – before you really do get stuck!

Wreck register: 108300171
Name: Unknown
Nationality: Unknown
Year built: Unknown
Type: MV Coastal tanker
Tonnage: 1,200 tonnes gross
Dimensions: L: 60m, B: 10m, D: 5m
Cargo: Ballast
Date sunk: May 1, 1986

On the deck, the oil transfer pipes run almost from the bridge to the bosun's storerooms forward, covering most of the available deck space. This is an interesting area to search for unusual marine life.

Marine Life

The marine growth has been slower to colonise this wreck than it has on others, but it began with the formation of some white coral patches on the deck and on the upper side of the hull. Covering large areas of the hull, these corals grow in circular patches about 100mm across. Hydrocorals,

looking like mini fir trees, have given the hull a dull light brown colour. On one of the walkways across the pipes, a colony of white soft corals has taken up residence on the treads and handrails.

Shoals of yellow coloured blackspot snapper swim over and under the labyrinth of pipes on the *Jasim's* deck hunting for their quarry. These little hunters are distinctively coloured and sport a black spot under the dorsal fins and longitudinal yellow pinstripes. They work equally well in packs, or on their own when they wait in the shadows for their dinner to come to them.

Heavy Metal
The high temperatures, humidity and salinity of the Gulf means that your dive gear will take a bit more strain than in other parts of the world. It's essential that you have your cylinders visually inspected once a year, and hydro-tested every five years here.

⌐ Aeolid nudibranch

Barnacles and sea squirts

Dive 10

Mariam Express

The newest arrival on the west coast, this wreck is home to unusual cargo and varied marine life.

Depth:	21m
Snorkelling:	No
Night dive:	No

GPS: N 25°27'19.7" E 55°06'16.0"

Distance from harbours:
DIMC 21.8nm @ 355° (175°)
Dubai Creek 14.7nm @ 316° (136°)

According to Lloyds Casualty Register, the *Mariam Express* was overloaded and sailing from Hamariyah to Iraq when she encountered strong winds and moderate seas. The vessel took on water and sunk rapidly. All the crew were rescued.

Diving

The *Mariam Express* lies on her port side with the bow facing 150°. At the time of writing, in summer 2006, the wreck was just a few months old but visibility on the site had been remarkably good, averaging 10m.

A buoy marks the aft section of the wreck. It's recommended that you go down the anchor and make your way to the bow. Inspect the bow area, then ascend a little to explore the hold. In one hold you'll find a number of tea sets all neatly packed in polystyrene, numerous bundles of quilt

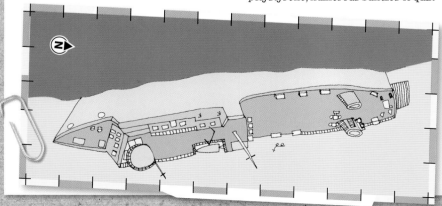

Oysters ↘

Wreck register: Not charted
Name: *Delos Express*
Nationality: Panamian, re-registered in France
Year built: 1978
Type: Roll-on roll-off vessel
Tonnage: 3,348 tonnes gross
Dimensions: L: 94m, B: 13m, D: 8m
Cargo: Household and electrical goods, scooters
Date sunk: May 2, 2006

bedding, and piles of electrical games scattered about. There are even couple of JCBs in one of the holds, along with twin tub washing machines and numerous scooters (one of which lies outside the hold).

When you're descending the anchor chain, you'll notice orange pieces of debris swaying in the current: this is the aft life raft which has been broken into three pieces, two of which are hanging on precariously. There's also plenty of debris on the seabed to pick over: rope ladders, tyres, broken crockery and so on. Don't forget to allow yourself time to inspect the masts and the deck railings. As the top of the wreck is at 8m, make the most of the dive and enjoy a last lingering look around while completing your safety stop.

Although a night dive on the *Mariam* would be possible, it's not recommended while there is any construction work in the area.

Marine Life

At the time of writing, the wreck had been down for a few months, but already boasted a variety of fish life. Large barracuda hang out at the bow of the wreck, enjoying the currents, while juvenile barracuda hide in the hold with the crockery and bedding.

The wreck is smothered with small oyster shells, and between the gaps you'll find numerous colonial ascidians or sea squirts in different colours – white, yellow, green, red or orange – as well as small anemones. The wreck also hosts the usual snappers, pennant fish and jacks. You may find a pair of resident sabretooth blennies, but their camouflage is excellent, making them difficult to spot.

Warning

As with any wreck, take care as you may cut or hurt yourself on jagged edges or protrusions. You should only try to penetrate the vessel if you're trained in wreck diving.

Crested sabretooth blenny ↗

Dives on Hold

While the developers of the offshore islands promise new dive sites, these old favourites are temporarily undiveable.

Some sites covered in earlier editions of the **UAE Underwater Explorer**, such as Rashid Wrecks and Jumeirah Artificial Reef, have been lost entirely due to construction

work on the island projects. Others, such as the four sites covered below, have been damaged, covered in silt, or lie in the path of construction shipping.

At the time of writing, in summer 2006, visibility in places was often down to less than a metre due to dredging operations. Anchoring and diving on some sites was hazardous and much of the marine life had disappeared. The hope is that the loss is temporary and that the sites will recover. Contact a local dive operator to find out when these four sites are worth diving again.

Car Barge & Tug

Depth: 20m

GPS: N25°16'16" E55°08'02"

Distance from harbours:
DIMC 10.7nm @ 356° (176°)
DOSC 7.4nm @ 321° (141°)

The Tug
Bow Facing 40°

33m @ 20° Route marked with pegs

N

Car Barge
Bow Facing 320°

The barge, sunk in 1986, is still virtually intact, and lies upright with her bow pointing north-west, at 320°. Her hold is filled with old cars and vehicle parts, and there's a small wheelhouse and cabin on the stern. At her bow a row of pegs runs for 33m to a small tug that was used for harbour work.

Diving

If you swim into the barge's cabin the noise of your breathing will be masked and your bubbles hidden, so you'll find that any fish on the site will start to close in. There are sections of debris to the north of the barge that the more adventurous can explore.

These two wrecks made for a good day dive and an excellent site at night, but are now heavily silted and will need time to recover.

DB1/SMB

Depth: 25m

GPS: N25°16'47.5" E55°03'44.5"

Distance from harbours:
DIMC 12nm 337° (157°)
DoSC 10.5nm @ 306° (126°)

80deg
75 m

Route marked
with steel pegs

The Derrick Barge (or DB1) was a purpose-built towing barge, completed on October 8, 1962. She had three decks, a helicopter pad on the stern and a 1,500 tonne American crane on the bow. DB1 is also known as Sheikh Mohammed's Barge (or SMB) as he agreed to the upkeep of the marker buoy in perpetuity.

The wreck was sunk by the UAE armed forces to form an artificial reef, along with a number of other surplus vessels and wrecks that form separate dive sites in their own right. She currently lies upside down in 23m of water on a flat, sandy bottom.

There are numerous holes in the wreck for the more adventurous to investigate. The DB1's hull is breaking up, and great care should be taken when exploring inside as parts of it are collapsing and there are many jagged edges.

A good dive plan would involve starting on the seabed after anchoring and then moving up the sides of the wreck looking for small creatures such as nudibranchs, crabs and shrimps. This way you'll end your dive on the upturned hull at 16m. Don't forget to leave enough air to do a safety stop on the anchor rope.

Diving

When good to dive, the DB1 is one of the most interesting of the wreck dives – and the site is so large that groups of divers exploring it at the same time often don't even encounter one another. It takes many dives to become familiar with the area and most people only have a clear understanding of what they have been diving on when the visibility reaches 15-20m. At the time of writing however, visibility was too poor to make the site worth diving.

DB1/SMB in her glory days ↰

Jaramac V

Depth: 23m

GPS: N25°16'49" E55°03'47"

Distance from harbours:
DIMC 12nm @ 337° (157°)
DOSC 10.4nm @ 305° (125°)
Dubai Creek 12.7nm @ 270° (90°)

The *Jaramac V* forms part of the large artificial reef around the Derrik Barge (also known as DB1 or Sheik Mohammed's Barge – see previous page) and is another of the sites that is not worth diving while construction on the islands continues. She lies 200m to the northwest of DB1 but is worth a separate dive when conditions are good.

Diving

The *Jaramac V* sits upright on the seabed and is more or less intact. She's an easy wreck to explore and you can access the bridge, engine room and accommodation quarters without too much effort.

This small wreck was visited even less frequently before construction on Dubai's offshore islands began, and while the construction continues, the poor visibility and construction shipping means that she's not worth the trip. However the payoff then was that she was home to larger marine life and hopefully once the islands have been built she will be so again.

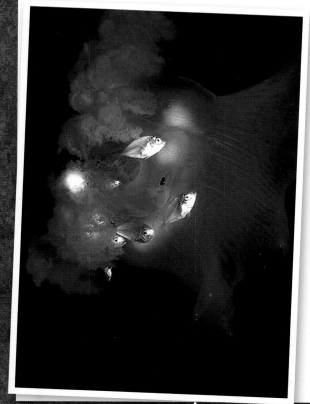

Juvenile fish catch a ride with a jellyfish

MV Sarraf Three

Depth: 20m

GPS: N25°16'07" E55°07'55"

Distance from harbours:
DIMC 10.5nm @ 355° (175°)
DOSC 7.3nm @ 319° (139°)
Dubai Creek 8.8nm @ 267° (87°)

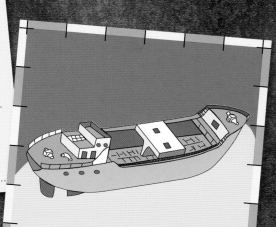

On the night of April 30, 1981, the Emirates coast was hit by a rare hailstorm. During the storm – in which golf ball-sized hailstones were recorded – the *MV Sarraf* was rammed by the *MV Taiser* while moored in Dubai. The *Sarraf* was raised that same year, re-floated and then abandoned in nearby Hamriya Port.

She was privately bought in August 1985 that year, then taken out and sunk at her present location. She lies upright and virtually intact (minus her brass fittings), with her bow pointing north.

Diving

Before the offshore construction work began, and when diving on this wreck was recommended, the site featured numerous, colourful soft corals and was an excellent site to explore at night.

Dive
11

MV Dara

The disastrous sinking of the *MV Dara* has resulted in a difficult, but rewarding wreck dive.

MV Dara in full steam

Depth:	20m
Snorkelling:	No
Night dive:	Yes

GPS: N25°34'29.0" E55°27'58.6"

Distance from harbours:
DOSC 27.4nm @ 28° (208°)
Dubai Creek 20.3nm @ 025° (205°)
Hamriya Harbour 5.8nm @ 347° (167°)
Sharjah Creek 12.5nm @ 19° (199°)

The *MV Dara* was a passenger liner built in 1948 by Barclay Curle & Co. of Glasgow, UK. Fitted with a single Doxford oil engine, she was operated by the British India Steam Navigation Company.

The story of the disaster is well documented. The following information has been compiled from *Last Hours on the Dara* by PJ Abraham, *The Grey-Widow Maker* by Bernard Edward and an article by Ian Bain that first appeared in the *Khaleej Times Magazine* of April 4, 1980.

The *Dara* sailed between Bombay, Karachi, the Gulf and the ports of Basra, Kuwait, Bahrain, Dubai and Muscat, carrying passengers, mail and cargo. During the early hours of April 8, 1961, after putting to sea on April 7 to weather out a storm, a bomb planted on her by an Omani rebel exploded. It's believed that the bomb was timed to explode when

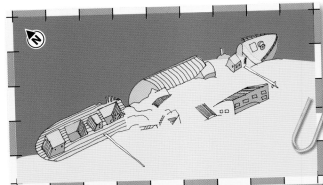

the *Dara* berthed at Muscat, but due to the storm, her departure from Dubai had been delayed. The bomb was planted to further the cause of the Dhofar rebellion; the uprising against Sultan Said bin Taimur, the rather erratic and isolated ruler of Oman, who was finally replaced in a bloodless coup by his son, the present Sultan.

The explosion between decks started a fire that raged for two days and caused considerable loss of life. The fire was finally extinguished, but the ship sank while under tow by *Ocean Salvor*, a salvage vessel. The final figure was 238 deaths; the second greatest number of fatalities recorded at sea in peacetime after the *Titanic* disaster.

The *MV Dara* is now owned by Clive Frost of Aqua Diving Services.

Wreck register: 108300171
Name: MV Dara
Nationality: British
Year built: 1948
Type: Passenger liner
Tonnage: 5.030 tonnes
Dimensions: L: 121m, B: 17m, D: 15m
Cargo: Mail and cargo
Date sunk: April 10, 1961

oxide from the rusting wreck, giving them a metallic reddish-brown colour.
The *Dara* also attracts many species of rays; shovelnose guitarfish, eagle rays and even feather tailed stingrays. The site is usually covered with snapper and, in the cooler months, barracuda, and it's occasionally visited by whalesharks.

Diving

The *Dara* lies on her starboard side at 20m, broken into three main sections. Every season the superstructure collapses further, limiting access to the wreck, although it is still possible to enter through the stern section.

This site can be quite dangerous as the tides can be very strong and visibility poor as a result. On a neap tide, though, this is an excellent dive.

Marine Life

One of the unique species of marine life that you're likely to see on this site are the cowries of the *Cypraea histro* and *arabica* varieties. Interestingly, their shells have absorbed the iron

Warty Doris nudibranch

MV Hannan

Practise your wreck penetration skills and hunt for warty Doris and other residents.

Depth:	20m
Snorkelling:	No
Night dive:	No

GPS: N24°50'11.0" E53°53'34.0"

Distance from harbours:
Abu Dhabi Club 33nm @ 306° (126°)
Jebel Ali Marina 62.5nm @ 260° (80°)

Given her position near the offshore rigs and platforms, it's logical to conclude that the *MV Hannan* sank while working in the Abu Dhabi oil fields.

Diving

The *Hannan* is a small coastal vessel that lies with her stern roughly pointing towards the north. Two buoys mark the site; the official cardinal wreck buoy, and a huge barrel with a large chain link that's anchored less than 3m from the stern on the starboard side.

Once you've descended, start from the seabed and go around the wreck in a clockwise direction towards the bow. You'll need to ascend a little in order to explore the hold area that's split in two by a small derrick. You can try some wreck penetration; you might be able to access the bridge and accommodation areas via a small window or via the companionway door. If you go through the door and out of the small window at the top of the wheelhouse, you'll find a small object that looks like a left-over treasure box.

Marine Life

As a result of the currents, you'll find large shoals of fish congregating on this wreck, including various species of jacks such as yellow striped jacks and finger jacks (also known as queenfish). The shoals share the currents with large, mean looking barracuda, some of which have unusual barred markings. The site is also home to some very big hammour that measure more than a metre in length, as well as large pufferfish and batfish.

Among the rays you'll see are bell, leopard, eagle and electric rays and guitarsharks. The rays are sometimes seen on the upper surfaces of the hull and companionways, looking for the nudibranchs that cling to the surfaces. If you join them, you may find

Wreck register: Not charted
Name: MV Hannan
Nationality: Unknown
Year built: Unknown
Type: Coastal vessel single screw oil engine
Tonnage: 288 tonnes gross
Dimensions: L: 42m, B: 6.5m, D: 2.6m
Cargo: None
Date sunk: August 3, 1986

one of the largest nudibranchs in the Gulf. Nicknamed 'warty doris', these creatures grow to about 125mm. Although it's large, warty doris is also well camouflaged and easily overlooked.

The site also has some inhabitants not seen regularly in the Gulf. There are small translucent colonial ascidians (delicate sea squirts) and an unusual purple soft coral that's formed in clumps all over the wreck.

Safety

The currents on this site can be very strong and as it's located well offshore, assistance may not be immediately available. You should also carry a dive knife or net cutters as this site is liberally covered with old nets.

Cool Critters

Some of the most colourful members of the marine world are the nudibranchs. The name translates into 'naked gill', and they either have their gills prominently displayed on their backs, or in a tuft at the posterior end.

As they're basically naked snails, nudibranchs have developed alternative defence systems. They're usually vividly coloured to try to persuade other sea life that they won't make a good main course. Many secrete a strong scent and others feed on sea anemones and hydroids – and use their lunch's stinging cells as their own defence mechanism.

Nudibranchs make excellent photographic subjects if you're into underwater micro photography – they're brilliantly coloured and not inclined to move very fast.

Dive 13

MV Ludwig

Once used as target practice, this wreck is now host to a growing marine community.

Depth: 27m

Snorkelling: No

Night dive: Yes

GPS: N25°06'53.8" E54°34'14.1"

Distance from harbours:
Abu Dhabi Club 37.3nm @ 15° (195°)
DIMC 31.2nm @ 271° (91°)
DOSC 35.3nm @ 262° (82°)
Jebel Ali Marina 26nm @ 286° (106°)

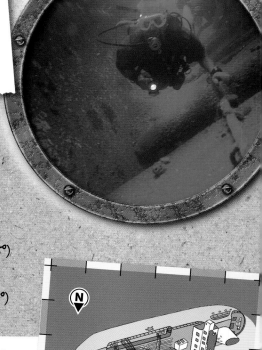

The *MV Ludwig* is more or less intact and lies on her port side, with her bow pointing east at 70°, in 27m of water.

The UAE armed forces used the *Ludwig* for target practice. The bridge received a direct hit and the explosion ripped out the internal walls and roof of the bridge. Damage can also be seen on the funnel, where shrapnel from the bridge punched holes in it. There is another projectile exit hole on the starboard side of the hull.

Diving

You can begin your exploration of the inside of the wreck via the bridge section, working your way down into the crew quarters or going through the stern hatches into the engine room.

The wreck is very similar to the *Lion City* (p.28), as the deck on both is a maze of oil transfer pipes and valves. You could almost be fooled into thinking you were diving the *Lion City*, as both ships were coastal oil tankers and both lie on their port sides. However, the MV *Ludwig* is larger and has two bridges over the pipe runs, as well as a small deckhouse forward of the bridge.

Marine Life

The marine growth on the *Ludwig* is relatively young, with hydrocorals and sea

Smelly Wetsuit Cures

Many divers have a warm-up trick that they'd rather keep quiet about. The evidence, however, lies in how their wetsuit smells . . .

Warming your suit 'the natural way' does provide a thermal boost, but it also allows bacteria to set up home in your wetsuit, and not even a good rinse can get rid of them.

There are a few products on the market that do help: the main one is called Sink The Stink, and it consists of a small capsule of deodorising liquid that's very effective at killing the bacteria and making your suit smell sweet (well, of neoprene) once again.

Shoals of yellow snapper

barracuda that constantly circle the wreck, while batfish live further out.

squirts being among the first inhabitants. The wreck's pipes and rigging offer security to a profusion of reef fish, like the shoals of pennantfish that glide over structures in close formation and the damselfish that dart in and out of the cover of the iron and steel.

A large resident shoal of yellow snappers seeks security from the hordes of

Wreck register: Not charted
Name: MV Ludwig
Nationality: Unknown
Year built: Unknown
Type: MV coastal tanker
Tonnage: 1,200 tonnes gross
Dimensions: L: 60m, B: 10m, D: 5m
Cargo: Ballast
Year sunk: 2000

Bannerfish

Nasteran

This site offers a good opportunity to practise your wreck diving skills... and to search for sea hares.

Depth:	23m
Snorkelling:	No
Night dive:	Yes

GPS: N25°28'00.0" E55°21'22.0"

Distance from harbours:
DIMC 25.2nm @ 028° (208°)
Dubai Creek 12nm @ 0.15° (195°)
Hamriya Harbour 7.4nm @ 262° (82°)
Sharjah Creek 5.6nm @ 341° (161°)

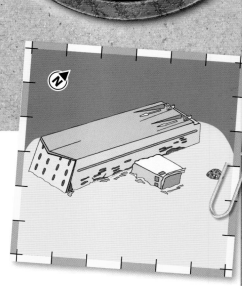

The *Nasteran* lies completely upside down in 23m of water, with her bow or landing door facing the shore at 150°. The wheelhouse lies to the east, next to the starboard side of the vessel, and both her propellers have been cut off.

Diving

Access to the accommodation and engine room is through a hole near the wheelhouse on the east side of the wreck, but note that this route is very silted.

The deck area forward of the wheelhouse is also worth a visit, but you'll need a torch to illuminate the fish life and marine growth.

Entry into the cargo area is through the partially open landing doors. If you're lucky, you could find some surprises in here, such as the blind juvenile sharks that like to hide in the darker areas of the vessel.

There's a lot of silt throughout the wreck, so pay attention to your finning techniques as you could easily reduce the visibility to zero. And if you're planning on penetrating the *Nasteran*, it's advisable that you use a line and torch at all times.

Marine Life

If you take the time to explore the upturned hull you're likely to be rewarded with the sight of many of the smaller creatures that are often overlooked; look out for shells, shrimps, nudibranchs, small blennies and unusual creatures called sea hares.

Sea hares are members of the shell family and are called 'hares' because of their

Sea hare

Wreck register: 108300201
Name: Nasteran
Nationality: Iranian registered
Year built: Unknown
Type: Landing craft
Tonnage: 652 tonnes gross
Dimensions: L: 62m, B: 10m, D: 8m
Cargo: Stones
Date sunk: March 14, 1970

rabbit-like appearance. They have two rolled rhinopores (sensory organs) on their head that seem to give them rabbits' ears, and two flaps, known as parapodia, to aid swimming. They are herbivorous and feed on algae and sea grasses – which means that the *Nasteran*'s hull is a regular smorgasbord for them.

Two strombus shells courting

Neptune 6

It's a long way offshore, but this is an excellent dive with the promise of 'treasure' to be found.

Depth:	25m
Snorkelling:	No
Night dive:	Yes

GPS: N25°30'22.0" E55°03'55.0"

Distance from harbours:
DIMC 25nm @ 349° (168°)
DOSC 21.5nm @ 022° (202°)
Dubai Creek 18.7nm @ 317° (137°)

Distance to other dive sites:
To Hopper Barge 6 (p.20) 0.18nm @ 43° (223°)
To Anchor Barge (p.6) 0.7nm @ 55° (235°)

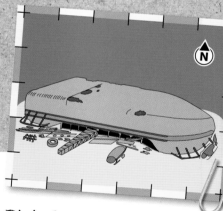

The *Neptune* was supporting the *WD Kent*, a drilling rig that was cross-drilling a burning oil well during one of the worst offshore fires that the Dubai Petroleum Company's Fateh Field has seen.

The *Neptune* pulled off during bad weather, but dragged her anchor and ended up colliding with the *WD Kent*, ultimately sinking the rig. After the collision, it was decided that the *Neptune* would be taken to Sharjah. However, she capsized while under tow and sank in her present position.

Diving

The vessel lies upside down in 25m of water with her bow facing 151°. There's a considerable amount of debris, including a crane boom, drilling equipment and wreckage from the deck accommodation, along her port side.

There can be strong currents at this site, making exploration quite difficult. For many years, the main entrance into the wreck

Octocoral

Wreck register: 108300055
Name: Neptune 6
Nationality: Panamanian registered
Year built: Unknown
Type: Drill rig tender barge
Tonnage: 2,300 tonnes gross
Dimensions: L: 79m, B: 15m, D: 8m
Cargo: General drilling equipment
Date sunk: November 12, 1973

was on the starboard side, a third of the way along the hull from the stern. Now that the wreck is breaking up though, access is possible on both the port and starboard sides, and you can swim all the way through.

Although this site is 18.7nm from shore, it's usually an excellent dive. There are also three other wrecks within a 1nm

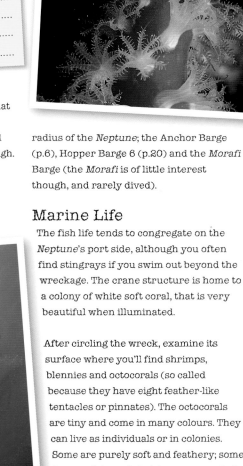

radius of the *Neptune*; the Anchor Barge (p.6), Hopper Barge 6 (p.20) and the *Morafi* Barge (the *Morafi* is of little interest though, and rarely dived).

Marine Life

The fish life tends to congregate on the *Neptune*'s port side, although you often find stingrays if you swim out beyond the wreckage. The crane structure is home to a colony of white soft coral, that is very beautiful when illuminated.

After circling the wreck, examine its surface where you'll find shrimps, blennies and octocorals (so called because they have eight feather-like tentacles or pinnates). The octocorals are tiny and come in many colours. They can live as individuals or in colonies. Some are purely soft and feathery; some have an internal skeleton composed of a type of calcareous material; and others still use another subject as a base from which to sprout. Take the time to watch their polyps pulse as they feed. The coral colonies pulsate at different speeds and the effect is quite hypnotic!

Up Close and Personal

Honeycomb moray ↘

Toby-fish ↰

Arabian stonefish

Up Close and Personal

Turtle

Frogfish

47

Dive 16

Swift

A deep and seldom-dived wreck with good marine life and the odd treasure still to be seen.

Depth:	38m
Snorkelling:	No
Night dive:	No

GPS: N25°27'37.7" E54°17'41.2"

Distance from harbours:
DIMC 51.1nm @ 294° (114°)
Dubai Creek 55.4nm @ 280° (100°)
DOSC 52.8nm @ 288° (108°)

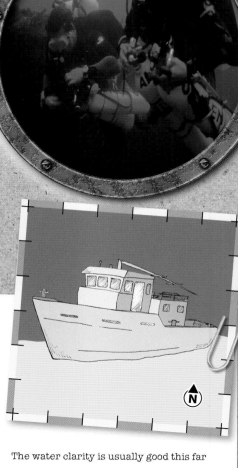

Swift sank following a collision with the Brown and Root pipe-laying barge No. 207, while working in the SW Fateh Oil Field. Today the vessel sits upright and intact on the sand, and stands 15m high in 38m of water. Her location is close to the Dubai Petroleum Company (DPC) and Dubai Natural Gas Company's SW Fateh oil and gas platforms.

Diving

This site is a long way offshore and is only occasionally dived, which is probably the reason why the fish seem almost tame. The wreck is located just 2.5nm (4.6km) away from the oil and gas platforms, so take care to keep to the south west of the oil field. DPC have strict procedures regarding access to the area. Unauthorised boats will be visited by the Coast Guard.

The water clarity is usually good this far out, and you can expect the visibility to be between 15 and 20m. When you descend, the first thing you're likely to see is the white soft corals that cover most of the wreck and give it an eerie glow.

There are several ways into the wreck for adventurous divers who are trained in wreck penetration. At times the wreck can be found draped in fishing nets, making

Wreck register: 10820202l (wreck no. 43707)
Name: *Claudine, renamed Swift*
Nationality: Bahraini
Year built: Unknown
Type: Motor tug
Tonnage: Unknown
Dimensions: L: 27.4m, B: 7.3m, D: 3.7m
Cargo: Unknown
Date sunk: February 21, 1987

access and exploration difficult. Ensure that you carry a small knife with you so that you're able to cut the nets if you get snagged in them.

Marine Life

The white soft *Telesto* corals (octocorals) are spectacular; they look like a blanket of snow that covers large sections of the vessel. Shoals of yellow and black striped jacks and snappers circle the wreck, parting and regrouping as you swim through them.

The marine life is well established and every surface is covered in layers of barnacles, oyster shells and hard and soft corals all competing for space. There are many holes and crevices for little creatures to dart in and out of, making this a very interesting dive.

Which One's Mine, Again?

Ever been on a busy dive boat and unable to find your gear because everyone's looks the same? A few minutes spent writing your name and mobile number on your equipment with a special marker pen will see you getting into the water first from now on.

And if you leave something behind or someone picks it up by mistake, you may even be lucky enough to get a phone call to set up a happy reunion.

Blubberlip snapper

Favites hard coral

Turtle Barge

An easy-to-access site that's home to fascinating corals, along with a friendly turtle.

Depth:	8m
Snorkelling:	Yes
Night dive:	Yes
GPS:	N25°26′43.2″ E55°26′57.6″

Distance from harbours:
Hamriya Harbour 3.1 nm. @ 226° (46°)
Sharjah Creek 5.2 nm. @ 39° (219°)

This is probably a small barge that's been scattered over a large area in three parts or large pieces of wreckage, but it could even be two small wrecks. The site was discovered by Blue Planet Diving in 1999 when divers were training outside the harbour wall in Ajman. The circumstances around the loss of the wreck (or wrecks) aren't known.

Diving

The wreckage lies just five minutes outside the Ajman harbour, so access is quick and easy and the site is excellent for night diving. As it is rather shallow it's also a good wreck site for snorkellers to explore. The wreck is fairly flat but full of holes that provide an ideal home for all kinds of marine life. A length of rope stretches about 60m between the two main pieces of wreckage to make navigation easier. There are some large pipes alongside one of the main pieces of wreckage and various bits and pieces littered about. It's easy to become

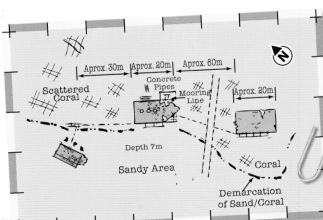

Wreck register: Not charted
Name: Unknown
Nationality: Unknown
Year built: Unknown
Type: MV coastal barge – single screw
Tonnage: Unknown
Dimensions: Unknown
Cargo: None
Date sunk: Unknown

disorientated due to the various pieces of debris, but as it's a nice shallow site you can simply surface and wait for the dive boat to collect you.

When diving here, please use the mooring buoy that Blue Planet Diving has created out of numerous bottles. This means you don't have to throw the anchor in and damage the corals.

Marine Life

As you descend the mooring buoy you'll be greeted by a lone clownfish who has made his home under the mooring line. And as the name suggests, you're also likely to encounter the friendly turtle that has take up residence on the wreckage.

This is an attractive site with an incredibly large number of hard corals spread over the seabed and wreckage. There are colonies of different coral families growing on top of one another, competing for space and light. If you look closely, you'll see the corals are almost fluorescent, and glow with hues of orange, green, red and blue.

The west coast regulars are all here: yellow snappers, blennies, monos, hammour and barracuda. You may also see nudibranchs, various types of sponges and shells.

This is an ideal site for students, and even well-dived instructors will find something to enjoy on this dive. If you're particularly keen to see many varieties of hard coral in a small area, this is a must.

Warning
Take care not to get your equipment or yourself caught on the wreckage and always wear protective clothing.

↖ Green turtle

Dive
18

Zainab

An interesting dive not only for Zainab's illicit past, but also for her present day marine life.

Depth:	30m
Snorkelling:	No
Night dive:	Yes
GPS:	N25°14'55.8" E54°51'32.4"

Distance from harbours:
DIMC 18.1nm @ 300° (120°)
DOSC 20nm @ 281° (101°)
Dubai Creek 23.8nm @ 265° (85°)

The *Zainab*, formerly called the *Seasroun Five*, sailed under a Georgian flag and was involved in the illegal transportation of light fuel oil from Iraq when she went down.

She was a general cargo ship with two holds forward and the machinery, bridge and quarters aft. To conceal her illegal cargo, her holds had been converted to hold the oil. She was carrying about 1,300 tonnes of fuel oil when she was deliberately sunk by her 11 man crew to avoid being boarded by the US Navy, who were enforcing UN sanctions on Iraq. The sinking resulted in a major oil spill on the northern Gulf coast, and caused serious concern to the local gas processing plant as she sank within a few hundred metres of their offshore gas pipelines. The story was documented by the *Gulf News* throughout April 2001.

Diving

The *Zainab* is intact and lies on her port side, the anchor still sitting snug on the bow. The covers of the holds are off and lie on the sea bed at about 30m. There are various bits and pieces of debris and artefacts strewn over the seabed; you'll find an empty compass binnacle, an upside down life raft at the stern and an industrial fire extinguisher on the seabed below the propeller.

The bridge, and the engine and accommodation rooms are easily accessible.

Fire fighting equipment

Wreck register: Not charted
Name: Zainab, originally known as The Seasroun Five
Nationality: Georgian registered
Year built: Unknown
Type: General cargo ship
Tonnage: 1,400 tonnes gross
Dimensions: L: 70m, B: 12m, D: 5m
Cargo: Fuel oil
Date sunk: April 14, 2001

But be sure that you can see daylight at the other end, before you enter the vessel.

This is one of the deeper dive sites on this coast and, at over 70m long, it's a fairly large wreck. You should be able to explore it in one dive though. A suggested dive plan is to start at the most interesting area, which is the now vertical deck. Make your way along the wreck and past the open hatches; their doors lie haphazardly on the seabed, looking like a discarded pack of cards. Investigate the upturned life raft when you reach the stern and, if you have enough time, take a look at the fire extinguisher that lies just beneath the propeller. Ascend slowly, exploring the bridge and decks aft. The remaining life raft is swinging from one davit. Go around the wreck and look at the propeller. Then return to the top of the wreck, at approximately 20m.

A night dive on the *Zainab* is possible for more experienced divers, but it's a long way offshore.

Marine Life

During the relatively short time the *Zainab* has been down, it has attracted a large variety of marine life. The wreck is carpeted with small oysters, and juvenile fish weave their way in and out of their shell homes. Most avoid contact with divers, but some are very inquisitive and allow you to get close to them.

You may find large rays resting on the seabed, and huge shoals of barracuda circling the wreck. You will often find large shoals of yellow snappers swimming round the various masts towards the bow, and there's usually a shoal of batfish that congregates near the bridge and wheelhouse.

Discover

MUSANDAM PENINSULA

- Modern dhows with A/C
- Day trips
- liveaboard trips
- Corporate events
- Fully equipped dive center
- Paragliding & Hang gliding

AL MARSA *Musandam*

Musandam

N

KHASAB PORT

KHASAB

20

25 24
23
39 22 32
27 36 30
29 37
28
35 40
26
34 31
33
38

41
45
42 44
43 21

SHAMS

ARABIAN GULF

MUSANDAM
(SULTANATE OF OMAN)

19

RAS AL KHAIMAH

UAE

GULF OF OMAN

BAYAH PORT DIBBA

DIBBA

© Explorer Group Ltd. 200

Musandam: Diving The Fjords

The Musandam has one of the most rugged, isolated and beautiful coastlines in the world; the towering Hajar Mountains rise directly out of the sea creating spectacular fjord-like scenery. There are endless possibilities for divers, and the sheltered bays also offer a safe environment for snorkellers and non-divers to explore.

The dive sites included in the book for this area are aimed at the more adventurous and experienced diver. Visibility is usually good – up to about 20m. The dives are all on the eastern coast and easily accessible from the UAE by dhow or motorboat, without the need to officially enter Oman. Sites like Lima Rock and Octopus Rock are some of the best locations that we have dived.

However, these sites represent only a portion of what is available in the Musandam area. The peninsula has a huge section of coastline, from Ras Al Khaimah in the north of the UAE, around Ras Musandam in the Strait of Hormuz, then down the east coast to Dibba, a small fishing village that's partly Emirati and partly Omani.

For divers there are two main ways to explore the area; either by boat up the east coast from Dibba or by driving to Khasab, the capital of the Musandam. It's always advisable to take your diving qualifications and some form of identification with you.

Dibba

By far the easiest way to dive the Musandam is to hire one of the dive boats or dhows operating from the east coast (most leave from Dibba Bayah Harbour). This way you don't need to get an Omani visa, even though, technically, you enter Omani territory. However you're not allowed to land. The boats operating in the area are Omani registered.

Trips can be booked through the dive centres, and, unless your operator has agreed to supply them, you will need to take all your own diving gear, including tanks.

To reach Dibba Bayah Harbour, which is in the Omani part of Dibba, you will need to first go through the UAE part of the town. No visa is required.

↖ White Rock aka 'Sydney Opera House'

Diving at Lima Rock ↘

Khasab

The other option for exploring the Musandam is to go overland to Khasab, via the west coast road through Ras Al Khaimah, and to contact one of the diving centres there (see the Dive Directory on p.181). You can take your own diving equipment with you, but dive tanks are sometimes refused entry, since the Omanis want to restrict diving to registered dive organisations.

To enter the Musandam Peninsula you will need a visa. Visa requirements depend on your nationality and whether you're a UAE resident or a visitor. Remember that regulations in this part of the world often change virtually overnight, so check details before you leave to avoid disappointment. There are UAE and Omani border posts at the entry point to the Musandam, so visitors will need the correct UAE visa in order to return to the Emirates.

If you have UAE residency and are on List 1 or 2 (see opposite), a visa can be obtained on arrival at the border. If you are not on either list, or if you're on List 2 and a tourist in the UAE, you will need to apply for a visa at the Omani Embassy in Abu Dhabi (02 446 3333) or the Consulate in Dubai (04 397 1000). The fee is Dhs.60. Visas usually take about four days to process, although sometimes the embassy or consulate is able to speed things up.

If you want to visit Oman more than once, a multiple entry visa is available at the border (for List 1 nationalities) or in advance from your nearest Oman embassy or consulate (List 2). The cost is RO 10, and the visa is valid for one year. Your passport must be valid for not less than one year at the time of applying. Holders of this visa can stay for up to three weeks at a time, but a minimum of three weeks must elapse between each visit.

The local currency is the Omani Riyal (referred to as RO or OR), which is divided

List No.1

Europe: Andorra, Austria, Belgium, Croatia, Cyprus, Czech Republic, Denmark, Estonia, Finland, France, Germany, Greece, Hungary, Iceland, Ireland, Italy, Latvia, Liechtenstein, Lithuania, Macedonia, Malta, Moldova, Monaco, Luxembourg, Netherlands, Norway, Poland, Portugal, Romania, San Marino, Slovakia, Slovenia, Spain, Sweden, Switzerland, United Kingdom and Vatican

South America: Argentina, Bolivia, Brazil, Chile, Colombia, Ecuador, French Guinea, Paraguay, Peru, Suriname, Uruguay and Venezuela

Other Countries: Australia, Canada, Hong Kong, Indonesia, Japan, Lebanon, Malaysia, New Zealand, Seychelles, Singapore, South Africa, South Korea, Taiwan, Thailand, Tunisia, Turkey and United States

List No.2

Albania, Belarus, Bosnia-Herzegovina, Bulgaria, China, Egypt, India, Iran, Jordan, Morocco, Russian Federation, Syria and Ukraine

into 1,000 baisa (or baiza). The exchange rate is usually about Dhs.10 = RO.1. However, dirhams are widely accepted in Oman.

Note that, by car, you can only enter and exit the Musandam on the Ras Al Khaimah side of the peninsula, not through Wadi Bih.

Night Diving

We have dived most of the sites mentioned in this area at night with great success. Less experienced divers may find the currents a greater problem at night than in the daytime.

You'll have to plan a night trip with your dive operator well in advance and expect to pay extra. Operators are generally less keen to arrange a night dive, unless you book an overnight trip or one lasting several days. In addition, unloading a boat full of dive gear late at night in Dibba Bayah Harbour with its high walls creates its own difficulties!

Operators

The number of operators that specialise in diving in the Musandam has grown in recent years (see a full list of operators on p.181). Al Marsa Travel & Tourism & Charters offer

Diver Safety

Remember the following points so that your Musandam dives are safe and pleasant.

- Follow the dive plan given by the operator, especially if it's your first time on the site and you do not have a dive guide with you.

- Be aware that the currents, upward and downward, can be challenging for even the most experienced of divers. Operators here usually run drift dives.

- It is recommended that you use an SMB (surface marker buoy). Many divers have a lot of fun with these, attempting to outdo all others with the most original SMB. Instead of buying an SMB from a dive shop, you can purchase all sorts of plastic toys and adapt them, but take care that your hand-crafted, and no doubt highly original, SMB doesn't fly away!

anything up to seven-day trips around the fjords on a dhow equipped for diving. *The Charlotte Anne*, which operates out of Dubai, also does liveaboard trips. Other companies such as Hormuzline, Khasab Dhow Charters, Khasab Travel & Tours, Musandam Sea Adventures and Nomad Ocean Adventures offer dhow cruises with stop-offs for snorkelling. Many operators will tailor make packages to suit you, but you may need to provide your own gear.

Extra Divers run a full service PADI dive centre at the Golden Tulip in Khasab, and many of the other dive centres, shops and clubs in Oman and the UAE also arrange trips to the Musandam.

If you want to take your own boat to the Musandam, you must seek special permission from the Omani Coastguard at Dibba Bayah Harbour coastguard post.

Teddybear coral ↗

See you at the border!

Whether you're visiting for the weekend or moving there for good, driving through the spectacular wadis or trekking in the Hajar Mountains, there's an Explorer product to help you make the most of Oman. Whatever you plan to do it's safe to say we've got the country covered.

Phone (971 4) 335 3520 · **Fax** (971 4) 335 3529
Info@Explorer-Publishing.com · www.Explorer-Publishing.com
Residents' Guides · Photography Books · Activity Guidebooks · Mini Visitors' Guides · Lifestyle Books · Maps

EXPLORER

Passionately Publishing...

The entrance to The Caves

The Caves

Great exploring and a wide variety of marine life awaits in these limestone caverns.

Other names: Khor Mala Caves

Depth: 10m

Snorkelling: Yes

Night dive: Yes

GPS: N25°48'14.4" E56°22'03.0"

Distance from harbours:
Dibba Bayah Harbour 10.5nm @ 028° (208°)

Distance from other dive sites:
From Lima Rock 9.9nm @ 212° (32°)
Ras Musandam 36.5nm @ 194° (14°)

Located about 500m from the pointed rock stack at Khor Mala, these caves aren't visible from the surface, but offer interesting diving in underwater caverns.

Erosion by the sea has cut these caves deep into the limestone rock face. The main chamber is an undercut section that runs about 15 to 20m into the rock. The bottom, at about 10m, is sandy and marked with boulders. There are several deeper caves at the back of the main chamber.

Diving

This is a good third dive of the day as it's shallow and doesn't go too deep into the rock face, making it ideal for those with a 100 or so bar of air left in their cylinders. A bright torch is essential for seeing your way, especially as this is a great site for peeking into holes and tunnels.

The site is also an excellent night dive as the rock offers some protection from the elements. Look out for all the crustaceans coming out to feed.

Snorkelling

Snorkelling here can be very good too. Swim along the rock wall and duck dive into the entrance of the cave – its roof is just above the surface of the water. A torch is necessary to make the most of this location and to see all the colours.

Marine Life

Enter the caves slowly, looking for stingrays and resting sharks on the sandy bottom. As you move into the caves, large shoals of golden cardinal fish will form curtains of red and silver as they guard the deeper crevices. The caves attract many varieties of small fish that seek the safety and food that these nooks and crannies offer.

Cleaner shrimps hide in the hollows. These white- and brown-banded shrimps can usually be seen by their tentacles sticking out of their hiding places. If you're lucky, you may spot some spiny lobsters hiding deep in the cracks.

Shrimp

A pair of sweetlips

The Landing Craft

A sheltered site that offers divers a chance to practise their wreck penetration skills.

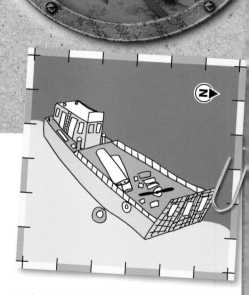

Depth:	10m
Snorkelling:	Yes
Night dive:	Yes

GPS: N26°12'40.0" E56°17'05.1"

Distance from harbour:
Khasab Harbour 3.5nm
@ 79° (259°)

This was a landing craft that specialised in carrying water to the villages that weren't able to receive water by road. The vessel was one of a fleet of three boats, each named after one of the villages they frequented with their essential load. The hull of *The Musandam* split with age, and it was decided that the vessel would be decommissioned. There was also a light aircraft that had been at Khasab Airport for about two years and the decision was made to load the plane onto the landing craft and take them out to sea to be sunk.

Diving

This small vessel sits upright and intact on the seabed at just 10m, with its bow facing 20°. *The Musandam* has a well-preserved and undamaged wheelhouse, which is surprising given that it's only 3-4m from the surface, and you can swim in and out of it easily. On a past dive, a prankster placed the loo on top of the wheelhouse.

You will be able to see the engine room through gaps in the deck, but it's a very tight squeeze and entry is certainly not to be attempted without adequate training.

Another interesting feature is the aeroplane laid out on the deck with its wings alongside.

```
Wreck register: Not charted
Name: The Musandam
Nationality: Unknown
Year built: Unknown
Type: Landing craft
Tonnage: Unknown
Dimensions: L: 35m, B: 7m, D: 3m
Cargo: None
Date sunk: 1990
```

You can see the propellers and the cockpit area with petrol tanks underneath what's left of the seats. At the front of the vessel is the landing deck which seems to attract a plethora of fish life. You can also find small bits and pieces of debris and tyres strewn about the wreckage.

After looking for shrimps, crabs and blennies in all the nooks and crannies on the wreck, take a swim over to the edge of the reef and look in the staghorn corals. You're likely to find a citron goby city in every coral you peer into.

This is an ideal site for students as it's on the edge of a protected bay with the rocky shoreline close by. Its proximity to the harbour (just 15 minutes away) means that it's also a quick and easy destination for a night dive.

Snorkelling

Snorkellers will enjoy this site too, as it's relatively shallow and it's possible to see the wreckage from the surface most of the time.

Marine Life

As the wreck has been here for several years, you'll see many shells and a variety of hard corals on it;

primarily brain and staghorn corals encrusted onto anything they can find: the wreck's surfaces, ropes, metal...

As Khasab isn't dived as much as other UAE sites, the fish appear to be quite unconcerned about divers and will swim almost into your face and regulator. Yellow snappers are always in abundance, especially in and around the landing ramp area. You're also likely to spot a couple of clownfish and anemone colonies.

Safety

This is a good site for students thanks to its protected position. You still need to take the precautions you would usually take when diving a wreck though, and watch that you and your equipment are not caught or cut on the rusty wreckage. It's also important that you wear protective gear.

Warning

Do not attempt to enter the engine room without adequate training. There's also a lot of rubbish in the form of rusted cans and broken glass lying around.

Diver in the wheelhouse

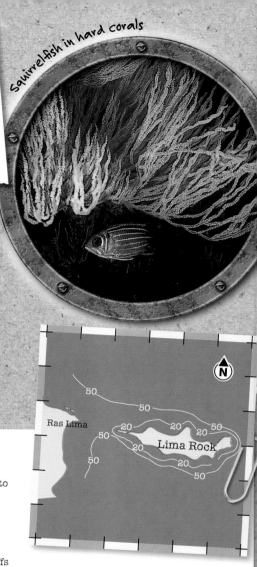

Squirrelfish in hard corals

Dive 21

Lima Rock

Boulders, limestone caverns, abundant reef life and a nearby island to chill out on.

Other names: Jazirat Lima, North and South sides

Depth: 12 to 60m

Snorkelling: Yes

Night dive: Yes

GPS: N25°56'27.2" E56°27'51.2"

Distance from harbour: Dibba Bayah Harbour 20.3nm @ 029°(209°)

Another great dive! Lying north of Dibba, Lima Rock, amid a plethora of coral and marine life, marks the southern entrance to Lima Bay. This small island is a pinnacle of limestone rock, about 800m long by 200m wide with steep, jagged sides. The waves have undercut the rock in places, leaving shallow caves and deep fissures. Sheer cliffs drop almost vertically to a depth of about 12m, then boulders and scree run steeply down to a sandy bottom at more than 60m.

Diving

The beauty of Lima Rock is that it can be dived in most weather and tidal conditions. If the sea is rough, or the current is running on one side, the other side is usually calm. Beware of the currents at the eastern and western tips of the island.

Snorkelling

Snorkellers will enjoy the site too and the north side of the island offers more shelter if you keep close to the rock face.

Marine Life

On the southern side of the island, there are a couple of relatively deep caves, one of which used to be the home of a 2.5m nurse shark, now only seen very occasionally.

At the south-eastern end of the island, a massive boulder guards the easternmost tip of the island. If the currents are mild, wait on this monolith and look out into the deep water for tuna, jacks, sharks and manta rays. If you're lucky you may even be rewarded with the sight of a whaleshark or a sunfish.

Between 12 and 20m, the boulder field is covered with hard corals (table, staghorn, brain and boulder coral), and patches of soft corals (orange and pink teddybear coral). The marine life is abundant, with large shoals of reef fish.

At 20m and deeper, abundant yellow and green coloured black coral, and numerous clumps of purple coral appear between the patches of sand, creating a very beautiful site. Look out for the yellow-mouthed morays that look as if they've just returned from the paint shop with their vivid, colourful markings. Moving deeper towards the shelving sand, white tip sharks and leopard sharks are often seen resting on the bottom.

On the north side, steep walls drop down to the sand at 20m. This side of the island is in shade from mid morning onwards.

The island is also home to a variety of birds such as ospreys, swifts and sooty falcons that frequent the high ramparts of the rock, making it an interesting location to wait between dives.

When Was That Again?

If you haven't been diving in a while – which means for more than six months – it's highly recommended that you take a scuba review or refresher course. Most dive centres offer them and you'll enjoy your next dive more, knowing that your skills have been refreshed and revised.

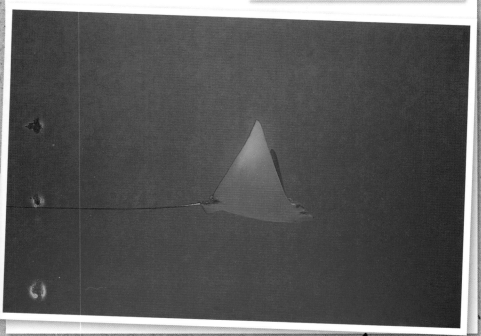

Eagle ray ↱

North of Lima

⤺ Diver on hard coral stack

Since the first edition of the **UAE Underwater Explorer**, it's become easier to travel and dive the spectacular northern tip of the Musandam, even the sites in the Strait of Hormuz. Several dive organisations and tour companies now operate in this area, offering magical trips.

The area is vast and with its memorable scenery, and many wonderful dives, it would take another book just to cover the Musandam Peninsula. Diving this area is very special, particularly as your chance of seeing many different types of sharks and larger fish is greater here than on other stretches of the coastline.

We have put together a selection of our favourite dive sites here, with a brief description of each. Over the years, the best sites have proven to be those around the islands, headlands and promontories. These rocky outcrops in the main current flow attract sharks, giant trevally, jacks, rays, shoals of tuna, dolphins and the occasional whaleshark. The strong currents washing over the corals keep them bright, colourful and healthy. The bays and inlets like Khor Habalayn, though calmer in rough weather, usually have slightly poorer visibility and there is less chance of seeing the bigger species.

The currents can be very strong so try to plan your trips to include sites where you can shelter from the current when it's running.

Bu Rashid

This is one of the larger islands in the Strait of Hormuz. The steep rocky cliffs drop down into the sea to a coral-covered shelf at 6m and continue on down to a wide shelf at 25 to 30m before dropping on to the shelving sand at 40m. On the north side is a wreck of a small fibreglass boat, and several species of shark are regularly seen here.

Other Name: Rashid's Father
Depth: 6-40m+
GPS: N26°24'12.0" E56°29'42.0"

Zebra shark

Depth: 16-50m+
GPS: N26°27'39.5" E56°30'57.2"

Jack patrolling the reef

Ennerdale Rock

This spectacular site is named after a bulk carrier that sank upon striking the rock. The rock, which is quite difficult to find – and to dive – is located in the main shipping channel where the currents can be fearsome, but the experience is well worth the effort.

The rock peak rises very steeply from the deep to a sharp point at 16m below the surface. We use a grappling hook on a shot line to get down to the rock, which glows out of the dark greenish-blue as you dive towards it.

The first things you'll see are the huge trevally and jacks that patrol the rock, and then myriad bright corals. The fish here are completely unafraid of divers and allow you to get very close.

Dive 24 Fanaku Island

Fanaku Island is the middle of three islands in the centre of the Strait of Hormuz. It consists of sparsely covered rock walls that descend in terraces. The currents can be very strong here and, being a small island, it doesn't offer any shelter. This means that only the smallest and strongest of marine growth manages to survive. This is definitely shark, jack and tuna territory and they can be seen on most dives.

Other Name: Gap Island
Depth: 6-50m+
GPS: N26°29'55.1" E56°31'50.4"

Dive 25 Great Quion Island

The northernmost island in Oman, Great Quion is the largest of the three islands in the main channel of the Strait of Hormuz and offers protection from the currents. The island's west side consists of gradually shelving rock, coral and sand. On the south and east side, cliff walls drop straight into the sea and then run steeply down in terraces.

The rocks and boulders on this side of the island are lightly covered in growth. From the northern point of the island, a submerged and narrow rocky ridge runs north east about 20m below the surface. Extending to 900m, this ridge drops very steeply to the west and is a favourite hunting ground for sharks, trevally and jacks.

Depth: 16-50m+
GPS: N26°30'21.0" E56°30'51.6"

↖ Spotted sweetlips

Dive 26 Hard Rock Cafe

This amazing rock pinnacle rises 8 to 10m out of the water, and looks as thought it's been twisted and had a rectangular block perched on the top. This is a shallow site of large, coral-covered boulders and patches of sand. You'll see huge shoals of reef fish, the variety and quantity of which is always surprising. This very colourful site is good for snorkelling, too.

 Snorkellers at Hard Rock Cafe

Other Name: Cork Screw Rock, Ras Bashin

Depth: 6-20m+

GPS: N26°12'13.0" E56°29'18.5"

Other Name: Horse Island

Depth: 6-40m+

GPS: N26°22'24.0" E56°26'51.0"

Dive 28 Jazirat Hamra & Dive 29 Jazirat Sawda

Jazirat Hamra (Red Island) and Jazirat Sawda (Black Island) are two islands that lie inside the sheltered bay of Dawhat Ash Shisah. A shallow shelving coral reef dotted with boulders surrounds both islands. The reef runs out into sand at a depth of 20m. Both sites teem with reef fish that dart in and out of the coral. Of the two sides, the east is dived more regularly.

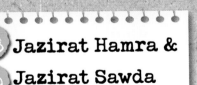

Dive 27 Jazirat Al Khayl

The deeper north side of this island is dived from the headland in the east into the bays, and along the north west headland. Steep cliffs and rock scree run sharply down into the sea to a coral covered shelf 6m deep. The boulder and coral slope steps down to a wide shelf at 25 to 30m, then drops on to the shelving sand at 40m. You'll see lots of reef fish here and perhaps even the occasional shark.

Other Name: Red Island and Black Island

Depth: 6-30m+

GPS for Jazirat Hamra: N26°16'54.0" E56°27'12.0"

GPS for Jazirat Sawda: N26°17'43.6" E56°27'12.5"

Dive 30

Jazirat Musandam East Head

When the currents are strong and the sea is a little rough, this headland and bay offer calm water and superb diving. At the point of the headland to the east, the cliff wall drops straight down to a depth of 50m. If you follow this wall into the northern bay, it gradually becomes a very pretty gentle coral garden slope, where a frenzy of reef fish feed. Sharks and schools of eagle rays may be seen rounding the headland.

Other Name: Picnic Bay
Depth: 6-50m+
GPS: N26°22'11.0" E56°32'18.0"

Other Name: Mother of Mouse
Depth: 6-50m+
GPS: N26°10'31.9" E56°32'47.2"

Dive 31

Jazirat Umm Al Fayyarin

The best areas to dive are the south bay and the east side of this island, but be aware that currents can be a problem. We recommend that you plan to dive this site when the currents are mild or running south.

Descending to 50m from the south east corner of the island is a rocky outcrop that separates its two dive sites. This rock attracts large marine hunters like jacks, barracuda and tuna, which can be seen hanging in the current. The east side dive consists of a magnificent reef of staghorn and table coral, dropping in steps from 6 to 20m, from the rock to the northern end of the island. The south bay consists of fallen rock covered in coral that descends to a sandy slope at around 20m. The sand continues downwards past 50m.

Dive 32 · Kachalu Island

Depth: 6-40m+
GPS: N26°23'45.5" E56°31'48.1"

Kachalu Island is one of the Musandam Peninsula's more popular sites, and it can be dived in moderate currents. The island's rock walls drop straight down to a shelf at 5m, then descend in steep steps to more than 50m in depth. One cave extends through the island and is nicknamed the 'washing machine' – for obvious reasons!

The walls are characterised by lots of gullies, holes and small shelves filled with hard and soft corals. Large shoals of fish frequent this site and whalesharks have also been seen here.

Dive 33 · Ras Dillah

Depth: 6-40m+
GPS: N26°07'51.0" E56°29'16.2"

Soft coral with brittle stars ↗

This dive site runs 500m into the bay from the north headland tip at the entrance to Khor Habalayn.

The sheer rock wall drops 15 to 20m to the sandy bottom, which is strewn with fallen boulders, and the seabed slowly slopes down to 40m. If you follow the sand all the way down and swim out a little, you'll eventually reach a depth of 40m.

The rock walls and boulders are covered in black coral. If it's sightings of the big pelagic fish you're after, they tend to gather around the headland. Note that this site is in shadow late in the afternoon.

Dive 34 Ras Dillah Ghubbat Ash Shabus Bay

Other Name: Lighthouse Rock
Depth: 6-30m+
GPS: N 26° 08' 37.3" E 56° 28' 47.1"

A tall peak resembling a lighthouse dominates this cliff-walled bay. Ospreys perch high above the water surveying the dive boats. Rocks and boulders have tumbled down into the sea and onto steeply shelving sand at about 20m, and if you swim out you'll reach a depth of over 30m.

You may see feeding stingrays filtering the sand, causing sand storms and leaving slight depressions on the seabed here. Undercutting of the rock walls and large boulders has created numerous overhangs and small caves (always good places to search for unusual marine life) while yellow and purple coral clings to the rocks. This is a colourful dive site with lots of large fish.

Dive 35 Ras Khaysah

This narrow rock promontory juts out into the sea for more than a kilometre and lies diagonally across the north and south running currents. One of the advantages of this site is that it offers diving in most sea conditions, so if the current is strong on one side it will be sheltered on the other. The terrain consists of cliff walls that drop to fallen boulders and coral at about 25m.

Depth: 6-25m+
GPS: N26°14'00.0" E56°29'24.0"

Other Name: Wall Street
Depth: 6-50m+
GPS: N26°23'12.1" E56°31'29.1"

Dive 36 Ras Musandam

This dive site is on the northernmost point of Jazirat Musandam, which is one of the largest islands in the area. The island's northern coast features high sheer cliffs that drop straight down into the sea to a narrow ledge at 6m. They continue to drop steeply down to a wider shelf at 25 to 30m and on to the shelving sand at 50m.

The strong currents have scrubbed the wall nearly bare of marine growth, and make for an excellent drift dive. Sharks, dolphins and whalesharks are seen here.

Dolphins are regularly spotted

Dive 37 Ras Qabr Al Hindi

This site extends from the easterly point of the peninsula, where the rocky bottom slopes to sand at 30m, to the south.

The area is a carpet of velvety coral with the occasional rock or boulder. Further south, the coral is not as abundant and the slope down to the sand is more gradual, with patches of sand starting at 10 to 15m. Rays and white tip reef sharks are often seen here.

Blacktip shark ↗

Other Name: Tip of the Indian Grave
Depth: 6m to 30m+
GPS: N26°18'33.8" E56°30'52.1"

Depth: 6-40m+
GPS: N26°05'17.3" E56°28'18.7"

Dive 38 Ras Sarkan

This dive site is around the headland on the south entrance to Khor Habalayn. The direction of the current will decide which side you will dive – but both are good. The site consists of fallen rock and coral with patches of sand below 20m. Try to make your way to the point of the headland and watch the trevally and tuna feeding in the main current stream.

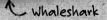

↖ Whaleshark

Dive 39 Ruqq Suwayk

This seamount or submarine mountain can be seen just below the surface of the water at 6m. The top of the mount is flat and covered with soft corals. Several gullies cut into the top of the rock and the sides step down in terraces to a depth of over 50m.

On the west side of the mount, you'll find a trail of debris, consisting of cargo (including calculators) from a wrecked dhow that lies at 40m. Several types of shark can be seen here gliding up out of the depths or just circling the seamount.

Other Name: Calculator Rock
Depth: 6-50m+
GPS: N26°24'11.9" E56°28'42.1"

Diver over corals ↗

Dive 40 White Rock

White Rock is a small island 500m to the north east of the Ras Khaysah promontory. The rocky sides of the island drop steeply down to depths of more than 50m. It's a small island and can easily be circumnavigated in a dive, and snorkellers will enjoy it too.

The sides are characterised by small shelves and fissures. Patches of coral nestle in these clefts and cracks and the smaller marine creatures cling to the shelter they find here. There are always large shoals of fish patrolling the island's outer boundaries.

Other Name: Sydney Opera House
Depth: 6-50m+
GPS: N26°14'11.9" E56°29'42.6"

Heavy Metal

The high temperatures, humidity and salinity of the Gulf mean that your dive gear will take a bit more strain than in other parts of the world. It's essential that you have your cylinders visually inspected once a year, and hydro-tested every five years.

Hitchhikers

Many juvenile marine creatures take shelter in the tentacles of a jellyfish, possibly for safety and the chance of any food scraps. It's not clear how they are immune to the jelly's sting though.

A juvenile filefish tags along

Porcelain crab hitching a ride on a jellyfish

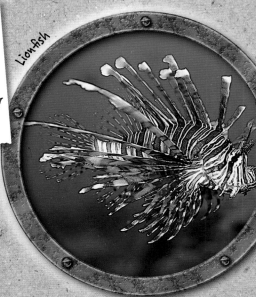

Lionfish

Octopus Rock

Another great Musandam dive, this site is practically a marine zoo.

Other names: The Stack

Depth: 5-20m

Snorkelling: Yes

Night dive: Yes

GPS: N26°00'01.2" E56°26'20.4"

Distance from harbour:
Dibba Bayah Harbour 23nm
@ 022° (202°)

With its distinctive undercut top, this isolated stack lies 3km offshore to the north of Lima and is another great Musandam dive site. The almost round rock is approximately 50m in diameter and its sides drop more or less vertically to a mixed rock and sand seabed.

The rocky bottom runs in ridges to the west and north, forming sandy-bottomed gullies. The depth of these gullies varies from 15-20m around the base of the rock, when they slope off to the southeast, descending more than 50m.

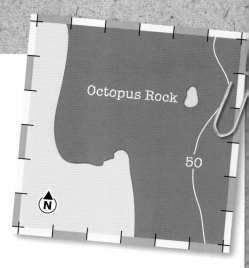

Octopus Rock

50

N

Diving

Octopus Rock is a marine zoo that can be enjoyed in most weather and tidal conditions, thanks to its sheltered location in Lima Bay. After reaching the bottom, swim north from the base of the rock and you'll reach a rocky cliff that runs east to west. This leads to the gullies, which are a continuation of the cliff. Most divers turn back at the cliff and circle around the terraces of rock that surround the stack. If you continue, remember to take note of your bearings, since you can end up a long way from the rock.

Snorkelling

Snorkelling is very good, especially around the stack. To make the most of this site you will have to duck dive down the sides of the stack. Alternatively, you can swim away from the stack to the north-west. There are large outcrops of rock 5 to 8m from the surface that are always alive with reef fish.

Marine Life

The stack is a gathering point for a great variety of shoaling fish life. Close to the rock you'll find numerous reef fish, while further out are jacks, trevally, tuna, barracuda and, if you're lucky, rays and sharks.

Soft and hard corals abound; green coloured black coral and purple soft coral whips predominate, and together with the pink and orange teddybear corals, they create a kaleidoscope of colour.

The rocks are home to fanworms, featherstars, juvenile crayfish and anemones. Look under overhangs and in hollows for black or red lionfish, but take care as these fish are poisonous. Stingrays can be seen feeding in the sand or resting under boulder coral overhangs on most dives. You also have a good chance of seeing nurse and leopard sharks on this site.

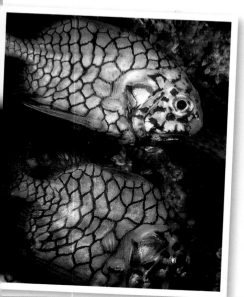

Watch your back

When you go snorkelling, you need to keep your skin protected from the sun – because you're in the water you often don't realize you're burning until it's way too late. Wearing a t-shirt isn't enough: it doesn't block out UV rays. You can wear a 0.5mm wetsuit or a shortie, or at the very least a rash vest. Whatever you choose, make sure you supplement it with plenty of waterproof sunblock, especially on your neck, ears, and the backs of your legs.

Pineapple fish ↱

Dive
42

Pearl Island

A great choice for a second dive of the day, this little gem offers snorkellers and divers plenty to see.

Other names: Oakley Island

Depth: 5-12m

Snorkelling: Yes

Night dive: Yes

GPS: N25°57'36.6" E56°25'51.9"

Distance from harbour:
Dibba Bayah Harbour 20.6nm
@ 031° (211°)

Distance from other dive site:
From Lima Rock 2.2nm @ 303° (123°)

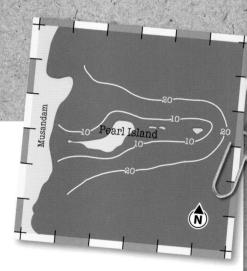

Located in Lima Bay, Pearl Island lies close to shore, just north of Lima. The water off the east tip of this rocky island is about 12m deep, and it gradually becomes shallower over the sand bar on the west side. Coral reef surrounds most of the island, descending gently from a depth of 5m to a sandy bottom at about 12m.

Diving

Since it takes about 50-60 minutes to swim around the island, and because of its depth, this site makes a good second dive with plenty to see. Corals run most of the way around the island and two rocks break the surface nearby. There's always a great variety of reef life here.

Snorkelling

The waters are usually very calm, making this a superb snorkelling site.

Marine Life

The reef is a mixture of hard and soft corals, with boulder, brain, cauliflower and daisy coral being the predominant hard corals, along with some orange and pink teddybear coral.

The island attracts a huge variety of small reef fish, and at certain times of the year, great colonies of murex shells can be seen mating and laying their straw-like eggs.

The first thing you'll hear as you submerge are the parrotfish crunching the coral. As you approach these pink, blue and green pastel coloured fish, they swim off leaving a trail of coral particles.

There are several patches of anemones dotted around the island, and almost each one is attended by its resident clownfish. If you're wearing brightly coloured gloves, especially yellow, and wave them near these little clowns they'll probably try to attack. The assaults are usually harmless (although for a small fish, they can deliver a nasty bite),

and the fish soon tire of the fun and return to the safety of their poisonous hosts.

The Fog

A foggy mask can really ruin a dive or snorkel trip. Most people have tried any number of things in diving lore, but we have two favourite tricks. The first is to rub a little toothpaste over the lens. This will get the fine layer of film off the mask (without damaging it) and it smells pretty good too. It's also a good idea to leave a little water in the mask until you put it on as this gets the mask to the same temperature as the sea.

If that doesn't do the job, try a squeeze of Johnson's Baby Shampoo in your mask and then rinse it just before you get into the water. And if you're not too thorough in cleaning the mask off, the beauty of it is . . . no more tears!

Whip coral ↗

Baby octopus in a shell

Dive 43

Ras Hamra

A shallow, colourful site with plenty of marine life, that's best dived in the early morning.

Depth:	5-16m
Snorkelling:	Yes
Night dive:	Yes

GPS: N25°55'20.7" E56°26'38.7"

Distance from harbour:
Dibba Bayah Harbour 20.4nm
@ 28° (208°)

This site starts at the point of Ras Hamra and runs west along the north cliff face. It's a north-facing site and lies in shade by the early afternoon, so to see this coral wonderland, you need to dive early in the morning when the sun illuminates it all.

Several large boulders break the surface near the headland, and the rest of the terrain consists of fallen rock and coral reef that drops to a sandy bottom.

The boulder coral on this site is extensive, running along the side of the cliff from 5m down to 16m, where the coral reef runs down to the sandy bottom.

Every available gap is filled with corals, from brain and daisy to tables of staghorn and great clumps of cauliflower coral fighting for space between the boulder coral.

Ras Lima

Lima

Lima Rock

Musandam

Ras Hamra

N

Diving

This is a shallow site with corals covering most of the fallen rocks down to a depth of 16m. When diving in these areas of hard coral, the sound of crunching fills your ears as the parrotfish munch away.

Snorkelling

This is an excellent site for snorkellers, as the reef starts at 5m, and you can see as much, if not more, than divers. Duck dive down and explore the corals, or simply drift over the reef and admire the display below.

Shrimp-fish

Marine Life

This is a good site for reef fish as there are lots of hollows and gaps where the fish dart in and out, playing hide and seek. You'll often see turtles resting between the clumps of coral.

Look into dark holes for the red striped squirrelfish that tend to wait in shoals under the overhangs and in dark corners of the coral. Little fish, with big eyes, they like to stay in the safety of the shadows.

Deeper in the water there are several species of grouper; some are brown with blue spots, others are red with blue spots.

Gliding over the tops of the corals are the real dandies of the reef; emperor angelfish, butterflyfish and bannerfish. Meanwhile, boxfish propel themselves like miniature hovercraft from one gap in the coral to the next. Then there are the solitary beauties such as the Picasso triggerfish.

You will also find crown of thorns starfish grazing on the coral here. When these voracious predators move on, they leave behind the bleached white skeletons of their former hosts.

Clown-fish and anemone host

When That Last Dive Was a While Ago

If you haven't been diving in a while – which means for more than six months – it's highly recommended that you take a scuba review or refresher course. Most dive centres will offer them and you'll enjoy your next dive more, knowing that your skills have been refreshed and revised.

The north face of Ras Lima

Ras Lima

Two sites for the price of one – and double the enjoyment for snorkellers and divers.

Depth:	5-16m
Snorkelling:	Yes
Night dive:	Yes

GPS: N25°56'46.2" E56°27'30.7"

Distance from harbour:
Dibba Bayah Harbour 18.8nm
@ 28° (208°)

The Ras Lima headland has two good dive sites for you to choose from; the north-facing site in Lima Bay and the east bay just south of the headland.

The north site is an interesting wall dive, with a steep cliff face that drops down to 10-15m in a tangle of fallen boulders. The east bay is located under the east headland cliffs. These are nearly vertical and plunge into the water to a depth of 6-8m where the coral reef gently runs down to the sand at 15m plus. Scattered throughout both sites are a number of large rocks, some of which form shallow caves.

Diving

The sites are in shadow in the afternoon, so plan to dive this site earlier in the day. Both locations can be explored in one trip, but it may be better to investigate each area separately. The headland divides the two sites, so if the tide and currents are running on one side, the other should be calm.

Whichever dive you do first, go down to the edge of the corals and the sand, then work around the bay to the headland. When the currents are mild, you can swim to the point of the headland and watch the shoals of larger ocean fish waiting to pounce on the reef fish. Close to the shore on the east bay, are some large boulder coral heads with undercuts and plenty of hollows.

Snorkelling

The east bay is an excellent site for snorkellers, with coral starting at 5m and some large boulders breaking the surface close to the shoreline. The boulders offer varied terrain and are in easy reach of all levels of ability. The north side of Ras Lima should only be attempted by more experienced snorkellers.

Marine Life

This is a good site for smaller reef fish and big pelagic fish. Manta rays have been seen here on several occasions, and the area is probably a cleaning station for them.

From 5 to 15m, corals cover most of the boulders that have fallen from the cliffs above. The boulder corals are large, with lots of cavities that make a perfect hideaway for fish like the blue triggerfish. Triggerfish

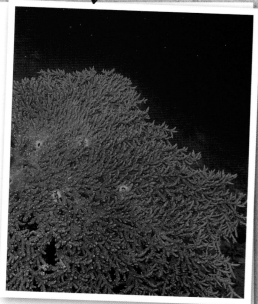

Table corals

don't seem to mind leaving parts of their bodies exposed when they are hiding, and you can often see bits of those distinctive, bright blue tails protruding from their hideaways when you're swimming overhead.

Stag and table coral fill the gaps between the boulder coral, but as you go deeper, teddybear and purple corals start to take over. At 12 to 16m you'll find yellow-coloured black coral that gradually gives way to the shelving sandy seabed.

Dive With A Torch

As you know, red is the first colour to disappear as you descend below 9m. Some divers only think to take a torch with them if they're diving on a wreck, a cave or planning a night dive. But we take a torch with us all the time: when you see a coral, turn on the light and see all the colour appear before you – like magic!

Batfish

Dive
45

Ras Marovi

These islands and channels make for a fun drift dive when the tide is running.

Depth:	6-30m
Snorkelling:	Yes
Night dive:	Yes

GPS: N25°59'06.0" E56°26'09.0"

Distance from harbour:
Dibba Bayah Harbour 21nm
@ 24° (204°)

A collection of four islands make up Ras Marovi. The two larger islands run in a line south-east from the mainland of Jebel Al Khatamah. The first large island is separated from the mainland by a 100m channel and the second large island has a 200m channel dividing it from the first island. The two smaller islands run south from the most seaward island. The cliffs of the two larger islands drop down vertically into the water. On the north face of the inner island, the wall is sheer all the way down to 30m.

Diving

The best diving is in the two channels. The depth of the channel nearest the shore varies from 30m to the north, rising up to 6m, and then dropping off to 28m in the south. The shallowest point of the second channel is 18m, dropping to over 30m on either side. The rocks and boulders slope down to a sandy bottom with a covering of both hard and soft corals. When the currents are running, drift dives through the channels can be great fun.

Snorkelling

Swim round the edges of the islands. At the deeper points you may see sharks gliding beneath you. The two smaller islands are great for seeing large shoals of fish, but it's well worth duck diving down and exploring.

Octopus ↘

hammour lie in wait for their prey. Leopard sharks, grey reef and white-tipped reef sharks and dolphins are regular visitors, while deeper down, stingrays rest on the sandy bottom. There have been several sightings of manta rays around the outer island.

Marine Life

There are lots of soft corals on these sites, including plenty of orange, pink and red teddybear coral. Purple and yellow coloured black coral is also prevalent.

The islands attract a lot of reef and pelagic fish. In the rock walls there are several shallow caves where large

The Ol' Fly & Dive

Combining diving and flying is always a little risky, so you should stop diving at least 24 hours before flying to give your body time to rehydrate and degas. Long flights should be avoided if possible and if you do drink alcohol during the flight you need to top up on even more water than usual to avoid becoming dehydrated.

East Coast

MUSANDAM
(SULTANATE OF OMAN)

Khasab
Ras Al Khaimah
Dibba
Dubai
Fujairah
Hatta
SULTANATE OF OMAN
Abu Dhabi
Al Ain
UAE
Arabian Gulf
Gulf of Oman

BAYAH PORT DIBBA
DIBBA

33

35
45
44

LULAYA HARBOUR
30

43
KHOR FAKKAN HARBOUR
31 29
34 36
39 41

42

MADHA (OMAN)

40

NAHWA (UAE)

MASAFI

UAE

GULF OF OMAN

38

FIMC
FUJAIRAH

37

32

KALBA

SULTANATE
OF OMAN

East Coast

Reefs, Wrecks & Rocky Islands

These maps are not an authority on international boundaries
© Explorer Group Ltd. 2006

East Coast: Reefs, Wrecks & Rocky Islands

Diving on the east coast is a very different experience to diving in the Arabian Gulf; while the west coast offers wrecks, the east coast is the place for divers seeking tropical marine life. However, the two wreck dives covered in the previous edition of the *UAE Underwater Explorer*, have since been supplemented by a third Inchcape vessel.

The east coast is affected by currents from the Gulf of Oman, the Arabian Sea and the Indian Ocean. These bring a multitude of exotic fish and most resident divers in the UAE would agree that the greater diversity of marine life makes this the most interesting side of the peninsula to dive. Depending on the moon's cycle, currents can sometimes be a problem, and dive operators will either anchor or carry out drift dives. The visibility is normally between 3 and 20m.

Night Diving

Night diving on the east coast is very rewarding as there's plenty of marine activity once the sun goes down. At this time, a lot of creatures that are shy and sensitive to light come out to play, and to hunt and feed. Other creatures tuck themselves into rock crevices, hide in shells or cocoon themselves in a thin, filmy 'blanket' to guard against being eaten while they sleep.

At night, many creatures also change colour and turn various shades of red in an attempt to camouflage themselves (the most difficult colour to see underwater at night is red). When you find one of these creatures and shine your torch on them, you'll see their true beauty. This amazing

Diver Safety

In order to make your east coast dives safe and pleasant, keep in mind the following points.

- If it's your first time on the site and you do not have a dive guide, follow the dive operator's recommended dive plan.

- Wear protective clothing for protection from the stinging hydrocorals found at some sites.

- At certain times of year there are small invasions of jellyfish – not all are of the stinging variety, but avoid finding out which are the hard way!

- Take a torch on the deeper dives. On sites like Coral Gardens, Anemone Gardens and Car Cemetery, the extra light will help you see the true colours underwater. And, of course, should you lose your buddy, the torch can be used for signalling.

- At many sites, especially Car Cemetery, you need to be aware of your buoyancy. This site in particular tends to silt up quickly, so control your finning techniques to minimise stirring up silt and clouding the water.

transformation applies to many species of fish and octopus.

It's advisable that you receive adequate training before your first night dive. It's also a good idea to dive with a minimum of three torches between two divers (ideally two torches each). Ensure you grease the rings correctly (if appropriate) and always use alkaline batteries for safety. Batteries never seem to last long underwater and torches are prone to flooding so it's wise to be prepared for the eventuality.

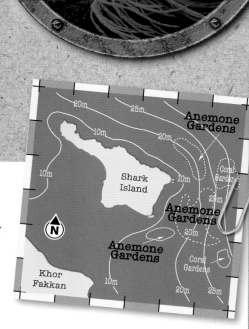

Diver and whip corals

Dive 46

Anemone Gardens

A beautiful site that makes a memorable dive, especially if you can spot an elusive seahorse.

Depth:	20m
Snorkelling:	Yes
Night dive:	Yes

GPS: N25°21'01.3" E56°22'46.9"

Distance from harbours:
Lulaya Harbour 2.7nm @ 179° (359°)
Khor Fakkan Harbour 0.9nm
@ 081° (261°)

There are many small sites within Anemone Gardens which is a soft coral reef on a sandy seabed, located northeast of Shark Island. You'll find a few metres of depth variation but it's fairly level. These sites are particularly pretty with plenty of green whip corals (which is actually a type of black coral).

Diving

The best way to dive this area is with a compass and computer. Keeping an eye on your bottom time, explore the dive site and search for the elusive seahorses that can occasionally be found here. Make your way back to Shark Island and as the reef becomes shallower you can have a safety stop, extend your dive time and admire the spectacular marine life.

The site is even more beautiful at night. The corals appear brighter by torchlight, and they will have their tentacles or polyps fully extended for feeding. If you're lucky, you may even see those seahorses with their tails wrapped around the corals, but you'll have to look closely because they blend in almost perfectly with their surroundings.

At night you're also likely to see moray eels swimming about in their search for food, and if you look up, you may even see squid. Squid are very inquisitive and are attracted to light – they sometimes become dazzled and swim directly into the torch beam.

At night it's particularly difficult to locate the anchor line for your ascent, so extra care needs to be taken. Always be aware of your depth, take a compass bearing and keep to the dive operator's recommended dive plan and time. The dive master needs to be vigilant too. It's best to anchor between Anemone Gardens and Shark Island, otherwise your time underwater will be further limited due to depth.

Snorkelling

Snorkelling is possible, especially on days when the visibility is 20m or greater.

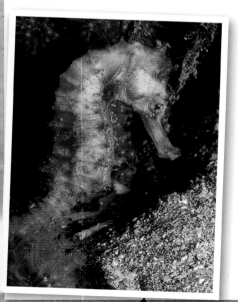

Seahorse ↗

But it's probably better to swim across to Shark Island (p.126) instead.

Marine Life

Shoals of several species of fish congregate around the island – from jacks and juvenile barracuda to fusiliers and small schools of squid. You will find hard and soft corals in a kaleidoscope of colours, especially orange and red teddybear corals. Wispy green whip corals sway in the current.

This is an excellent dive spot that offers divers an opportunity to spot a shy seahorse – search carefully but if you find them *please do not touch*.

Dive With A Torch

As you know, red is the first colour to disappear as you descend below 9m. Some divers only think to take a torch with them if they're diving on a wreck, a cave or planning a night dive. But we take a torch with us all the time: when you see a coral, turn on the light and see all the colours appear before you – like magic!

Car Cemetery

A site to test your navigation skills – with the reward of some unusual marine life.

Depth:	18m
Snorkelling:	No
Night dive:	Yes
GPS:	N25°25'07.0" E56°22'34.2"

Distance from harbours:
Luyala Harbour 1.6nm @ 24° (204)

As the name might suggest, Car Cemetery is a graveyard for wrecked cars that was created in about 1988 to form an artificial reef and a special site for fishing. There are about 200 vehicles here and the nucleus of the site covers an area of about 60 square metres.

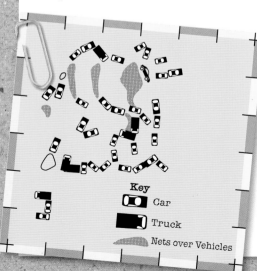

Key
Car
Truck
Nets over Vehicles

Note that the map below only depicts the main cluster of car wrecks.

Diving

Due to the flat seabed and the lack of any distinguishing features on the car, this is a difficult site, both to find and to navigate around. Visibility is also usually poor as the site is located near a wadi entrance.

There's also a lot of sediment in the area, so take care to keep your buoyancy in check, otherwise you will be down to zero visibility! In the daytime, you tend to meander from one wrecked car to another, looking in the distance for the shadow of the next vehicle. At night though, you won't be able to do this and you'll need to rely on your compass.

Although not frequently dived in the dark, Car Cemetery makes a memorable night

dive. Corals come out at night extending their polyps to catch and feed on micro-planktons. We've also encountered several unusual and light-sensitive nudibranchs that aren't seen in the daytime. There's also a beautiful sand anemone that we've seen at this site. During the day it's nondescript and looks a bit like half a tennis ball. But at night it extends itself to feed and resembles a head of celery decorated with baubles. Once a photo is taken, the bright flash from the strobe forces it to retract.

Due to the openness of the area, which is at the mercy of the wind and currents, this is a tricky site to navigate around at night, but it's not impossible. You will need to arrive in daylight and position yourself correctly, then wait for darkness. The dive operator should be prepared to up-anchor to collect you, as it's likely that you'll struggle to find the anchor rope for your ascent.

Marine Life

Most of the cars are covered with algae and fishing nets, some of which have fishing pots on them. Since the visibility is usually poor, it's best to take your time and look for smaller creatures, such as shrimps and Omani clingfish hiding among the featherstars. This site is considered a nudibranch haven and you'll find numerous species on the wrecks and discarded fishing nets.

Look carefully for seahorses and frogfish, as well as small manta rays and the occasional spotted eagle ray. There are also two large resident honeycomb morays that measure about 2m each on these wrecks.
Don't dismiss this site because of the low visibility; persevere, look closely, and you never know what you might find.

Honeycomb moray eel ↖

Purple whip coral

Coral Gardens

Resplendent with colourful corals, this is a great night dive for experienced divers.

Depth:	26m
Snorkelling:	No
Night dive:	Yes
GPS:	N25°21'12.0" E56°22'48.0"

Distance from harbours:
Lulaya Harbour 2.6nm @ 179° (359°)
Khor Fakkan Harbour 1.1nm
@ 81° (261°)

Coral Gardens is one of the deepest sites on the East Coast and can be an interesting multi-level dive. It consists of a soft coral reef on a sandy seabed and it's located on the north-eastern side of Shark Island.

It's difficult to pinpoint it unless you follow the correct bearings closely, but if you miss the exact location, don't worry; simply follow the compass bearing back to Shark Island and you'll encounter smaller, shallower reefs on the way. The area is resplendent with green coloured black whip coral.

Diving

As this is a 'flat' site, we suggest that you follow one of the following two dive plans (opposite), preferably with a dive computer. The site is prone to both

thermoclines and unusually strong currents. Do not attempt Dive Plan 2 if there's a strong current running. We also suggest that this site is only suitable for more advanced divers with a minimum of 30 dives behind them.

Coral Gardens is a beautiful night dive. The corals are out feeding, nudibranchs are hunting and molluscs, crayfish

(map showing Shark Island, Khor Fakkan, Coral Gardens, Anemone Gardens with depth contours 10m, 20m, 25m and N compass)

and crabs are on the march at an incredible speed.

However, this is a deep night dive and fairly 'open', so adequate preparations and planning are vital. It's imperative that you take the time and depth into consideration and decide on contingency plans prior to your dive. Finding the anchor at night is tricky, but not impossible. In case of difficulty, you could navigate your way over to Shark Island, or surface slowly, shining your torch up towards the surface.

Citron goby

Snorkelling
Coral Gardens is too deep for snorkellers – rather head over to Shark Island.

Marine Life
This location has some unusual soft corals that we haven't seen on other dives. In particular, the delicate soft dandelion coral is fairly common here, as well as clumps of green wispy whip coral. During the winter months, you could be lucky enough to see razorfish (also known as shrimpfish), swimming upside down and darting from one clump of coral to another. You may also see guitar sharks, and large crocodilefish, with their big flat heads, crocodile shaped mouths and beautiful eyes with frilly eyelids. Seahorses are seen here occasionally, but they are becoming increasingly rare.

Dive Plan 1
Stay on the dive site proper, but watch your bottom time and give yourself a good safety stop. This is the plan to follow when the current is strong.

Dive Plan 2
For a multi-level dive, explore this site for a maximum of 10-15 minutes (or according to your dive computer), then follow a compass bearing back to Shark Island. You'll find that your bottom time increases as you follow the reef up to 13m and arrive at the base of the island, usually within 30 minutes. This allows you more time to enjoy the site, as well as to have a good safety stop.

Don't forget to tell the dive operator what your dive plan is!

Shrimp on a starfish

Dive 49

Deep Reef

A deep, but attractive coral plate reef with interesting sea life.

Lionfish

Depth:	30m
Snorkelling:	No
Night dive:	Yes

GPS: N25°04'02.7" E56°24'25.6"

Distance from harbours:
FIMC 4.53nm @ 141°

Distance to other dive sites:
To Refinery Reef (p.124) 14.3nm @ 355° (175°)
To Inchape 10 (p.114) 3.8nm @ 341° (161°)

When Scuba International opened their new dive centre from Fujairah Marine Club, they researched the area and, with the help of some of the local fishermen, located this reef in late 2001. They have since buoyed the largest of these coral plates to make locating the reef quick and easy, ensuring that you have the maximum amount of time in which to enjoy this picturesque site.

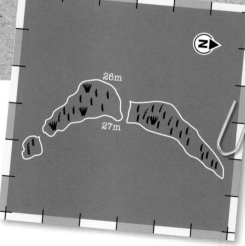

Diving

Just a 15-20 minute boat ride from Fujairah International Marine Club (FIMC), this deep and flat dive site ranges from 28-30m in depth, depending on the tide. The area consists primarily of a sandy seabed and several large slab-like plates that dot the contourless sandy bottom and rise up about a metre from the seabed.

Marine Life

As the plate coral rests almost a metre above the seabed it attracts shy marine life: morays who like to hide under the shaded plates and shells keeping themselves out of direct sunlight. If you look closely, you will see shrimp dancing to attract fish to their 'free' cleaning service. It's a very pretty site with various displays of soft corals; green whip or black coral, large branching bottlebrush corals, teddybear corals in various colours and several types of sea fans. All of these corals are in excellent condition due to the strong currents that flow through the area bringing it a rich supply of nutrients. They seem to have lined themselves up, row by row, and where one fan ends, another strategically places itself close by to ensure that every nutritional morsel is absorbed from the water.

Most noticeable here is the abundance of an unusual orange sponge. It's quite unknown from any other site and it looks a bit like spiky chimneys. You will find the usual East Coast sea life here: barracuda, turtles, seahorses, snappers, hammour and box fish. Sharp-eyed divers will spot moses sole and rays resting camouflaged on the sandy seabed.

If you are fortunate you may encounter sea snakes here. Admire from a distance as sea snakes are extremely venomous. Rather enjoy watching them poke their heads under the ridge in search of snacks.

Safety

As it's a deep site, you need to take care on this dive and the use of a computer is highly recommended. If you're trained in the use of Nitrox this will help you to maximise your dive time.

Nitrox Diving

Several dive centres offer Nitrox training, (see the Dive Directory on p.181) as does the Desert Sports Diving Club for its members. You can get Nitrox fills and cylinders from Scuba Dubai, DSDC, Scubatec, Sandy Beach Hotel, and Scuba International. Remember to take your N2 diving card with you for proof of certification.

Find out more about furthering your dive training on p.144.

Green turtle

Dive 50

Dibba Island

A site with colourful corals, where you're virtually guaranteed a sighting of a turtle.

Depth:	16m
Snorkelling:	Yes
Night dive:	Yes

GPS: N25°36'14.1" E56°21'05.9"

Distance from harbours:
Dibba Bayah Harbour 5.2nm @ 122° (302°)
Khor Fakkan Harbour 15.2nm @ 353° (173°)
Lulaya Harbour 12.8nm @ 347° (167°)

This small rocky island has long sloping sides that are covered by a reef formed by a variety of soft and boulder corals. The side nearest the shore is only 3-4m deep, so it should be dived at high tide. The seaward side has a long sloping rocky reef with many green and purple whip corals that make it a very attractive dive site. Some of the staff at the Holiday Beach Motel have been very proactive in protecting Dibba Island and have placed several mooring buoys around the island. Please make use of them as dropping your anchor could damage the corals and reef growth.

Diving

If you're in a hurry, it's possible to complete a circuit of the island in one

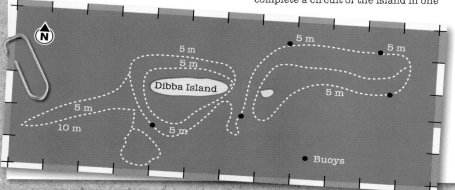

N

5 m
5 m
5 m
Dibba Island
5 m
5 m
5 m
5 m
10 m
5 m

• Buoys

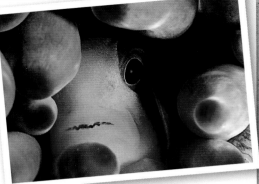

dive, but only at high tide. Regardless of the tide, if you're planning several dives in this area, it's a good idea to explore the wall that runs parallel to the island. The area is prone to both thermoclines and strong currents.

At low tide we recommend you keep to the north (seaward) side of the island, otherwise you'll be snorkelling, instead of diving, on the south (shore) side. At high tide we suggest that you explore the side of the island that's nearest the mainland. There's a good chance you'll see turtles there.

Dibba Island makes a lovely, easy night dive, and is simple to navigate. There are lots of beautiful, swaying corals that will have their polyps out to feed at night, and you'll find sleeping fish that have lodged themselves between the rocks, often leaving their tails exposed. You may also come across sleeping turtles: do not touch or disturb them as they're easily alarmed. They could actually swallow too much water in their fright and drown. And if you don't disturb them, you'll have more time to examine them close up – a wonderful experience!

Snorkelling

This is one of the best snorkelling sites around, especially for seeing turtles. The turtles are most prolific on the seaward side of the island where there are lots of coral reefs, and it seems that snorkellers will see turtles, even when divers don't. Swim to the island if you are a strong and proficient swimmer, or go by boat for safety.

Marine Life

You're virtually guaranteed sightings of turtles on this site and you'll see many fish species here too. Look out for the unusual jawfish (or hole goby), noticeable for their rather ugly features – huge heads and large eyes and mouths. They build lovely 'drainpipe' homes, and line the walls with pretty shells to prevent them from collapsing. The drainpipe goes down quite a long way and once the jawfish disappears into it, it takes a long time to reappear. When it's mating season (usually June to August, but it seems to depend on the water temperature), they pop out of their holes, exposing their colourful and beautifully patterned bodies.

Be careful of the resident clownfish – they are sometimes rather aggressive, bashing your mask with some force and giving your fingers a nip!

Jawfish with eggs ↗

Dive
51

Hole in the Wall

A rocky coral wall that makes a great dive at night, when it's a haven for sleeping fish.

Boxfish

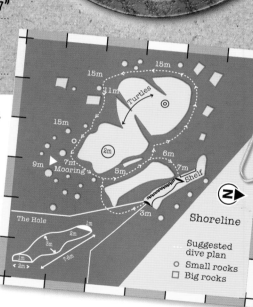

Depth:	15m
Snorkelling:	Yes
Night dive:	Yes

GPS: N25°20'26.3" E56°22'39.7"

Distance from harbours:
Khor Fakkan Harbour 2.9nm @ 118° (298°)

The site is close to where a fuel depot is being constructed and, due to the fact that the mountain behind this area is being levelled to make a harbour, the site still suffers from excessive silt and poor visibility. However, since the completion of the main excavation work, the site does seem to be starting to recover.

Diving

This site consists of a rocky coral outcrop that slopes out to sea.
It has a small swim-through that's just large enough for divers to get through comfortably, but considering the visibility on some days, it's not surprising that not everyone finds the 'hole in the wall'!

However, there's a mooring buoy at one end of the submerged rock and if you follow the coral outcrop around to the point where you can swim between it and a second small outcrop, you're on the right track. Continue around the back of the rock until you find yet another outcrop. When you're at about 7m, you should be able to find the hole: it's about 1.5m in diameter at the entrance and it opens up a little more as

Map labels: 15m, 15m, 11m, Turtles, 15m, 2m, 6m, 9m, 7m Mooring, 5m, 7m, Shelf, The Hole, 1m, 3m, Shoreline, N, 2m, 3m, 1m, 2m, 7.8m

Suggested dive plan
○ Small rocks
□ Big rocks

you swim through it. The swim-through is about 8m long and varies between 1.5 and 3m in diameter. It's large enough to swim through comfortably, just so long as it's not lined with urchins, and you will see little beams of light coming through a crack in the roof of the rock.

At night this is a haven for sleeping butterflyfish and parrotfish. You need to be in control of your buoyancy though as at night the urchins tend to seek you out to inflict their worst on you.

Snorkelling

It's a shallow site and, even if the visibility is poor, snorkellers will enjoy some interesting marine life, particularly if you snorkel close to the wall.

Marine Life

You'll find all the usual east coast underwater creatures here, along with small shrimp enjoying the ride and meals courtesy of some fat pincushion starfish. Look out for purple finger corals beautifully decorated by brittlestars – it looks a bit like the corals are wearing colourful striped scarves. Take the time to peer between all those urchins and see if you can find an elusive needleshrimp, difficult to see because they blend in with the urchin spines. Turtles are regularly seen here, often with remoras clinging on to their shell. Cuttlefish and batfish seem to be prolific for most of the year, and you might find small stingrays in the middle of the swim-through.

Safety

This site is renowned for its sea urchins, so take care with your buoyancy. Also keep an eye out for the bryozoans; they look small, harmless and fern-like, but these tiny creatures deliver a powerful, irritating sting. If there's any surge or waves on the day you're diving, select another site as this is not one to dive in inclement weather.

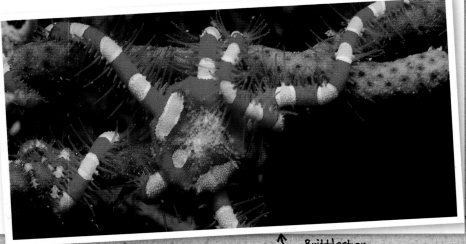

Brittlestar

Inchcape 1

A decommissioned boat that's become home to a wide variety of marine life.

Depth:	32m
Snorkelling:	No
Night dive:	Yes

GPS: N25°30'44.8" E56°22'56.7"

Distance from harbours:
Khor Fakkan Harbour 10nm @ 13° (193°)
Lulaya Harbour 7.2nm @ 15° (195°)

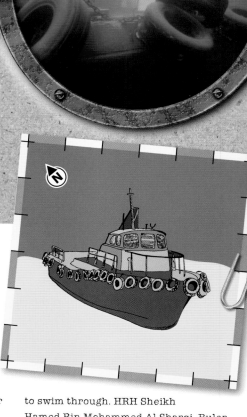

Inchcape 1 - originally known as *Gray Swift 2* - was built in the USA by Halter Marine and shipped to Dubai in 1971 or 1972. She started her service in Ras Al Khaimah and in 1991 moved to Dubai where she was renamed *Inchcape 1*. She was used by Inchcape Shipping Services to transport crew and supplies to and from ships, oil platforms and rigs in both Dubai and Fujairah, and was decommisioned in 2001. General Manager Eric Laing and his colleagues, Captain Joe Finch and Louise Marr of Inchcape Shipping Services decided that the decommissioned boat would be ideal to sink and form an artificial offshore reef.

The engines were removed and cleaned of oil residues, and the doors and hatches were taken off to allow divers to swim through. HRH Sheikh Hamed Bin Mohammed Al Sharqi, Ruler of Fujairah, member of the Supreme Council, granted permission for the boat to be sunk. Finally, and with the assistance of Dibba Municipality, Sandy Beach Motel, Sandy Beach Dive Centre, Al Boom Marine and Inchcape Shipping Services, the boat was relocated to her final resting place.

Diving

This is a small vessel that sits upright and faces south. There are car tyres around the gunwales, and a couple of the hatches can be found on the seabed at the stern of the wreck.

The depth of this dive can be over 30m, depending on the tide. The wreck is small and it's possible to go around it several times during a dive. The best plan is to swim around it slowly, starting from the seabed. After searching for the many residents hiding between the hull and seabed, ascend to the deck area where you can explore the holds and the engine room.

You will need a light to reveal the colours of the marine life seeking the sanctuary of these dark spaces and, with a bit of a squeeze, access into the wheelhouse is possible. You can then go up to the top of the wheelhouse and on to the navigation mast to enjoy the last few minutes of the dive, before ascending and completing your safety stop.

Wreck register: Not charted
Name: Inchcape 1 originally known as Gray Swift 2
Nationality: United Arab Emirates
Year built: 1971
Type: Steel crew boat
Tonnage: 57 tonnes gross
Dimensions: L: 21m, B: 5m, D: 3m
Cargo: None
Date sunk: December 12, 2001

Whip goby ↗

Cardinalfish

Marine Life

Although this is a relatively new wreck site, the fish world took up residence on it very rapidly. You can find large rays hiding under the wreck towards the stern. A large shoal of cardinal fish takes up all the space in the safety of the wheelhouse, trying to avoid being eaten by the large barracuda and emperor fish that cruise around outside, waiting for an easy meal.

You will see large hammour and several species of moray eels hiding in the tyres. Look out for yellow-mouthed moray, pennant fish, boxfish, soldierfish and red bigeyes. The fish life is attracted by the spreading algae. There's a large blenny that lives in the navigation box, and if you look closely you will see many species of nudibranchs. There are more and more fish beginning to congregate on this wreck and you never know what you'll find here!

Going Artificial

The benefit of sinking an old vessel, or even an obsolete rig, is that it provides a habitat for hundreds of underwater species to live and feed on. This is generally a positive change, especially where the seabed is largely flat and featureless. It's no guarantee that a wreck will become a healthy and diverse reef, but the chances are that nature will snap up the opportunity. Turn to 'A Year In The Life Of *Inchcape 2*' on p.111 to read an account of a wreck's gradual transformation into a reef.

Warning

Be aware that with depths of up to 30m, this is a fairly deep site and the currents can be quite strong.

Big eyes

Fish Eyes

← Peacock flounder

Torpedo ray →

Parrotfish

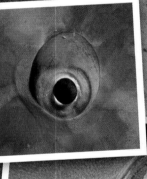

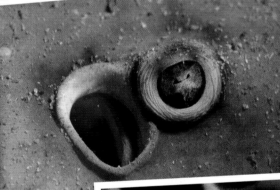

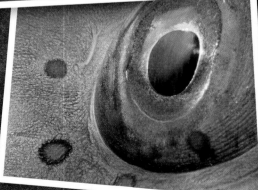

Broomtailed wrasse ↑

← Honeycomb moray

Dive
53

Inchcape 2

Practise your wreck penetration skills and explore this rich marine habitat for its treasures.

Depth:	22m
Snorkelling:	No
Night dive:	Yes

GPS: N25°20'19.8" E56°22'53.3"

Distance from harbours:
Khor Fakkan Harbour 1.8nm @ 108° (288°)
Lulaya Harbour 3.4nm @ 167° (347°)

The boat was built in the USA by Halter Marine and shipped to Dubai on a Hansa Line vessel in 1974, where she started her service before being moved to Fujairah in 1991. She was renamed in 1993 and eventually relocated to Ras Al Khaimah in 1995. She transported crew and supplies to and from ships, oil platforms and rigs during her working life.

Although she had just received a new coat of paint, it was found that she needed considerably more work to make her seaworthy, so the decision was made to decommission her. The artificial reef created when Inchcape 1 was sunk was so successful, and the marine life it attracted in a relatively short time so prolific, that it inspired the Inchcape team, Eric Laing, Captain Joe Finch and Louise Marr to offer Inchcape 2 for the same purposes. The wreck was sunk in shallower waters to make it accessible to the majority of divers.

The boat was moved to Fujairah where she was prepared for her new life underwater. It took more than two weeks to ensure she was clean of oil residues, and the doors and hatches were removed to enable divers to swim through the wreck safely.

Diving

The *Inchcape 2* sits upright in 20-22m with the bow facing 90°. You'll find debris around the wreck; the engine hatch doors, other doors and a few of the wheelhouse's shattered glass windows that were pushed out with pressure as the wreck sank.

It's possible to enter and swim through the whole wreck, end-to-end, but take care as some of the internal fittings have become loose with age. Entry to the engine room can be gained through the aft deck hatches. Swim through the living quarters, past the bathroom and when you've seen enough, you can exit via the stairs at either side of the wreck. If you're more adventurous and of medium build, you can exit through the bow hatchway. Take care if you choose this route; while it's quite easy and safe, you need to ensure that your equipment doesn't get snagged.

Inchcape 2's deck

Wreck register: Not charted

Name: *Inchcape 2* originally known as *Gray Lance*

Nationality: United Arab Emirates

Year built: 1971

Type: Steel crew boat

Tonnage: 57 tonnes gross

Dimensions: L: 21m, B: 5m, D: 3m

Cargo: None

Date sunk: April 24, 2002

Divers looking into the wheelhouse

Marine Life

The wreck is located between Martini Rock (p.118) and Anemone Gardens (p.92). The abundant fish life of these two sites has spread quickly to occupy this new habitat. Already there are rays, moray eels, juvenile barracuda, jacks and cardinals benefiting from this new wreck.

During the initial months of its underwater incarnation, the wreck was covered with small white anemones, that carpeted the decks and railings, giving it a ghostly glow, and jewelled anemones. Various sponges, young teddybear corals, encrusting worms and algae have also rapidly taken over the wreck and are enjoying their new home. There have been some sightings of frogfish and seahorses, but these come and go.

The best way to enjoy this wreck is to go down the buoy line, currently connected to the port side of the stern. Move slowly around the vessel and explore the seabed; you'll probably find some large jawfish hiding in the debris. You may be able to make out the loading marks with numbers on the bow, although these are now encrusted with calcerous worms and various algae and bryozoans.

What's The Weather Like?

The UAE Meteorological Department provides a good overview of the weather on www.uaemet.gov.ae with up to 48 hours of accurate predictions. One useful section is Marine, where they give current data on sea conditions and time tables for all over the country.

Once you've made your way around the wreck, ascend to the deck area through the engine room and swim along to the bow. Alternatively, you can look in from the outside. Shine your torch inside the engine room and you'll find lots of juveniles hiding between the engine parts and pipes. The wheelhouse is spacious and you can easily enter and exit through the gaping holes.

Jewel anemones

A Year In The Life Of Inchcape 2

An artificial reef sounds like a contradiction in terms. But when manmade objects are cleaned of their residues and toxins, and deliberately sunk, marine life is often quick to take up residence. This is an account of how the sea and its inhabitants came to call *Inchcape 2* home.

Within the first two months of *Inchcape 2* being sunk on April 24, 2002, the first marine organisms began to make an appearance. Small limpets and barnacles started to take hold of all the surfaces, and were followed shortly by small algae and seaweed growths. Next came the calcareous tube worms that made pretty patterns all over the ship's blue paintwork.

This activity and growth increased over the next two months and suddenly it seemed as though the wreck had developed a thick carpet of algae, anemones and tusk-shaped worm tubes.

The fourth month also saw small teddybear corals starting to take shape like little snowballs scattered over the

Algae growth ↗

'Snowballs' on the deck

appearance, possibly attracted by the algae and bryozoans that were growing well at this stage. Some strange spaghetti-like algae also appeared.

This continued into the eighth month. The sponges were growing well and small gobies began to take up residence inside them. By now, the wreck was covered in feather stars and for several months there was the strange phenomenon of clouds of non-stinging jellyfish that hung around the site.

Three frogfish appeared on the wreck in its ninth month as an underwater habitat. These must have been the most photographed frogfish in the world as for most divers in the UAE this was their first opportunity to see a frogfish up close. They hung around for a few months and then disappeared. They haven't been seen since. The wreck continued to flourish with 'mushroom' jellyfish flying like UFOs over

deck. By the fifth month, the fish world had discovered the wreck. Fish, invariably snappers and batfish, started to gather in large shoals – in fact, you sometimes couldn't find the wreck for the fish! The teddybear corals, sponges and algae had grown considerably by this time too.

From the seventh month onwards, an even more varied amount of marine life was found. Small blennies took up residence in some of the pipes and small cowry shells camouflaged themselves on the teddybear corals. Around about this time, nudibranchs made an

Decorator crab on teddybear coral

Teddybear coral

Underwater Photography

A site like *Inchcape 2*, with its many tiny marine creatures, is just the kind of dive that's likely to spark off an interest in underwater photography. Those frogfish and decorator crabs lend themselves to macro, or close-up, photography, which is often the route that most people follow when embarking on this new passion. And with digital cameras and underwater housings, photography is an aspect of diving that is rapidly becoming more accessible to people.

Underwater photography is not simply photography that takes place under the surface of the sea, though. Even professional photographers find themselves struggling to adapt to conditions underwater. There's the water to contend with for starters: water refracts light, is full of little particles that show up as a snowstorm on your pictures, and it absorbs colour. To counter the effects, you need to get as close as possible to your subject, and you'll need to learn how to use flashes (called strobes). Getting up close to that nudibranch also requires excellent buoyancy control – it's no use photographing the reef's rich marine life if you're bumping into it and destroying it as you go along. It's also a tricky thing learning to master your equipment, let alone diving with it. Using it and setting up a shot while maintaining your buoyancy becomes an art in its own right.

That said, with a little practice and the aid of the many underwater photography courses that are on offer today, this could be your next big thing – turn to p.148 for more information on how to get started and what sort of equipment you will need. The sense of accomplishment when you get that perfectly framed shot is addictive and you'll keep coming back for more.

the site, and numerous varieties of crabs, crayfish, squat lobsters and decorator crabs becoming regular sightings. Divers can count on it being encapsulated by shoals of snappers.

Coming up to the anniversary of the wreck sinking, it was now entirely covered with some sort of growth; algae, teddybear corals, whip corals and hydrozoans, all of which was inhabited by crabs, lobsters, shells and nudibranchs.
Diving on the *Inchcape 2*, whatever the season, always provides something interesting and different for the photographer and diver.

Anemones

Dive 54

Inchcape 10

An always-varied and interesting site for trained wreck divers.

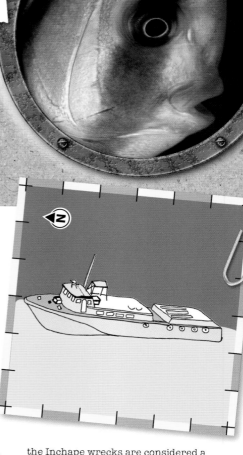

Bat-fish

Depth:	24m
Snorkelling:	No
Night dive:	Yes

GPS: N25°07'36.1" E56°23'05.3"

Distance from harbours:
FIMC 1.53nm @ 90° (270°)

This is the third ship Inchcape Shipping Services has sunk to form an artificial reef (see p.104 and p.108). As ISS is a Fujairah based company, special permission was sought from the authorities and HH Sheikh Hamed bin Mohammed Al Sharqi, Ruler of Fujairah, member of the Supreme Council, gave his approval for the project.

The boat, originally named *Jetwise*, was built in Singapore in 1982 and was initially owned by a company in Bahrain. ISS bought her in 1998 and she was moved to Fujairah where she transported crew and supplies to and from ships and oil rigs. What makes her unusual is that she was propelled by three water jets.

As with the other Inchcape wrecks, ISS spent a considerable amount of time and money ensuring the boat was environmentally friendly and equipped for her new life underwater. On the whole,

the Inchape wrecks are considered a success as they've attracted an incredible amount of marine life within a relatively short period of time, and they've taken the burden off some of the other dive sites.

Diving

This is the largest of the *Inchcapes* and she sits upright at 24m with the bow facing north. You should consider penetrating the

Wreck register: Not charted
Name: Jetwise
Nationality: United Arab Emirates
Year built: 1982
Type: Steel crew boat
Tonnage: 84 tonnes gross
Dimensions: L: 27m, B: 6m, D: 4m
Cargo: None
Date sunk: June 28, 2003

This is an easy site to get to for a night dive, thanks to its proximity to the harbour. But take care if you've already completed a dive or two during the day as your bottom time may be limited. It's quite an eerie night dive, but you'll see creatures that you don't normally spot in the daylight like morays, crabs and shrimps.

Marine Life

Since this wreck was purposely located close to another artificial reef, the fish have homed in on it. In its first few months it acted as a nursery and you could find most species of fish in miniature on it; banner fish, hammour, lionfish, snappers, jacks, filefish, morays and a juvenile snake. It became covered in a layer of hairy, dark red or brown algae and some small calcerated worms began to encrust the surface areas, particularly on the windows and other glass bits. Since it's still a relatively new wreck, the marine life on it is constantly changing and every dive holds another interesting discovery.

Safety

You need to use dive tables or a computer on this dive; it's a square profile and time is limited. Make sure that you descend and ascend the buoy rope and always complete a safety stop. As with all wrecks watch out for sharp edges that might cut or snag you.

vessel only if you are a trained wreck diver. If so, you can enter from the engine room at the back and swim through the living quarters and up one of the sets of stairs.

The best way to enjoy this site is to go down the buoy, connected to the starboard side of the stern, slowly work your way around the wreck and explore the seabed where you may find some rays resting. Once you've gone around it, enter the wreck (with the above caution in mind) and ascend to the deck area through the engine room. Alternatively, you can swim around the deck perimeter and shine your torch inside the engine room, wheelhouse and crew quarters to spot the many varieties of juvenile fish that stick closely together in small shoals.

The wheelhouse is easily entered and exited and while you're there, you should take a look at the ship's horns on the wheelhouse roof which always seem to stay reasonably shiny and algae-free. You can then move up to the upper deck area where you can play with the controls. Swim over to the mooring rope for a nice slow ascent, remembering to complete a safety stop.

Blenny

Ines

A deep, technical dive that makes a good entry-level option for Trimix divers.

Green whip corals

Depth:	72m
Snorkelling:	No
Night dive:	No

GPS: N 25°11'21.8" E56°27'30.6"

Distance from harbours:
FIMC 6.2nm. @ 62° (242°)

While the *Ines* was anchored about 13km off Fujairah in August 1999, there was an explosion on board that resulted in a fire. Five crew members were reported missing, two were injured, 22 rescued and there was one fatality.

Diving

The DSDC Dive Club has buoyed the wreck with a buoy 1.5m under the surface, which is attached at the other end near the propeller. There appears to be a thermocline anywhere between 9 and 30m on each and every dive made on this wreck. The thermocline temperature can change by up to 5°C and can create a thick sludge of bad visibility. Once you're underneath the thermocline though, the visibility is usually very good.

As you reach the bottom of the anchor rope you will be at a depth of 55m. This is where the propellers are, as the

wreck is completely upside down. You can then proceed to the seabed at 70-72m and start to work your way around the wreck.

As she lies upside down, the structure of the ship has been destroyed but there are one or two areas where you can go underneath her and come out the other side. You can see some portholes

Wreck register: Unknown
Name: *Ines*
Nationality: Belize
Year built: April 1967
Type: Oil barge/tanker
Tonnage: 6174 DWT
Dimensions: L: 112m, B: 15.8m, D: 6.9m
Cargo: None
Date sunk: August 9, 1999

a relatively short time. Then start your long, slow ascent making the necessary decompression and safety stops using the relevant air mixes.

Marine Life

This wreck is not dived as often as other dive sites, due to its depth, and the fish life varies according to the time of the year you visit it. Still, you're likely to encounter jacks, tuna, rays, guitar shark, hammour, cutlass fish, barracuda and cuttlefish.

amidships towards the stern and some railings are visible. On the ship's starboard side you'll find a large sunken mooring buoy full of tyres.

It is possible to go inside the wreck down the corridor, however, it's imperative that you're aware of your surroundings and bottom time at all times. The bow is damaged and it appears that this is where most of the explosion and fire damage happened. You can then work your way from 70m back to the prop at 55m by swimming up the hull, which is sprinkled with soft and hard coral growths, and you will notice some anodes still visible even though the wreck's been down there for

For Technical Divers Only

This dive is not for sport divers as it's considered too deep for compressed air diving. *Ines* lies at 70m+ and it's imperative that you're trained to dive at this depth as it's outside what is considered safe for sport divers.
Ines is however, a good entry level dive for Trimix diving (see the write-up on technical diving on p.145).
All divers should be familiar with decompression diving with a Nitrox mix for decompression and able to deploy an SMB from blue water in an emergency. With this type of diving it is also imperative to have various safety measures - safety divers, oxygen cylinders and so forth - on board.

Dive 56

Martini Rock

A pleasing and colourful site that makes you feel like you're diving in an aquarium

Teddybear corals

Depth:	3-22m
Snorkelling:	Yes
Night dive:	Yes

GPS: N25°20'05.2" E56°22'53.0"

Distance from harbours:
Khor Fakkan Harbour 2nm @ 122° (302°)
Lulaya Harbour 3.6nm @ 179° (359°)

Martini Rock

Martini Rock is a small, submerged coral outcrop, the top of which is visible from the surface at 3m. The rock has several sandy gullies or alleys and most of it is covered in orange and purple teddybear coral, which makes for a pleasing and colourful dive site. This is an excellent site for divers of all skill levels, and a favourite east coast location.

Diving

The north side of the rock is the deepest, going down to 22m, while the rest of the site is at about 13m. There's enough time to complete a circuit of the rock in one dive, but note that the site is prone to both thermoclines and strong currents at times.

The variety of fish life is excellent and the top 5m is like an aquarium – schools of snapper, fusiliers, anthias, triggerfish and large-mouth mackerel are present for most of the year.

Martini Rock is an excellent option for a night dive, although if you don't know the site well, navigation may be a problem. You may see sleeping turtles, rays out feeding and perhaps a spotted eagle ray. At night the rock appears completely

red because of all the feeding teddybear corals. Look closely into the soft corals to find fish, such as juvenile damselfish or hawkfish, that use the coral as a safe haven from the larger hunters that are out looking for dinner. If you stay near the bottom of the rock on the seabed, you may see large rays sifting through the sand in search of small molluscs and crustaceans. They will come right up to you at night and can cause quite a scare!

You may also encounter large pufferfish that swim about at night completely oblivious of their surroundings, bumping around rather as if they were in a pinball machine! Don't shine your torch at them for too long, as they'll become completely disorientated.

At night you could come across a strange looking fish called a long finned waspfish (a type of gurnard). They appear to run over the seabed on three spider-like legs, that are hidden underneath their winged fins. They have two pronged feelers extending from their mouths that they use to search for creatures hidden in the silty seabed.

Snorkelling

For snorkellers, this is a great, rocky, shallow location that teems with life. The top of the rock is about 2-3m from the surface (depending on the tide), and the bright colours of the teddybear corals decorating the rock are easily seen. You may also see boxfish, jacks and many shoals of fish near the surface. If you can duck dive down to 5m or more, you may see morays, rays and perhaps a turtle.

Marine Life

Large sections of the rock are covered in red, purple and orange teddybear corals, with one side swathed in purple whip corals, and green and yellow whip corals in a deep corner. There are also clumps of featherstars that hide shrimps, Omani clingfish and nudibranchs.

You may be fortunate enough to see the occasional leopard shark, black tip reef shark or guitar shark. We've also found some unusual creatures; a pygmy seamoth, frogfish and a robust pipefish. The sight of these unusual tropical creatures here in the UAE caused great excitement.

Warning

During their mating season (June to August), the red tooth triggerfish that you often find on this site become particularly territorial. They tend to dart towards you at a fast pace, only to turn away at the last moment with millimetres to spare. We suggest you heed their warning and swim by quickly!

Murbah Reef

A shallow reef full of vivid corals and curious fish.

Hammour over coral reef

Depth:	5-14m
Snorkelling:	Yes
Night dive:	Yes
GPS:	N25°16'21.0" E56°22'31.6"

Distance from harbours:
FIMC 14.3nm @ 6° (186°)
Khor Fakkan Harbour 8.2nm @ 171° (351°)
Lulaya Harbour 8.4nm @ 175° (355°)

Distance from other dive sites:
From Ras Qidfa (p.122) 3.1nm @ 187° (7°)
From Refinery Reef (p.124) 1.1nm @ 196° (16°)

This is another of the sites Scuba International discovered, this one in the summer of 2001. What sets Murbah Reef apart is that it's covered with hard corals all competing for space – in fact, it's difficult to see the seabed thanks to the dense coral growth.

Diving

The reef stretches for about 400m along the coastline. At 5-14m it's ideal for the last dive of the day or for beginners with excellent buoyancy control. If you're diving the site at night, we recommend that you arrive at the reef just prior to sunset so that you can anchor in a sandy patch and wait for darkness. The site is quite noisy at night, thanks to all the corals that become active after dark. You'll see various shrimps, crabs and morays, and possibly even a sleeping turtle.

Snorkelling

The site is very attractive and shallow enough for snorkellers even when visibility isn't great. It's an excellent

spot to find small fish hiding in the corals, and it's also good to see so many healthy hard corals thriving at this shallow depth, especially when you consider the wide range of water temperatures here.

Marine Life

The attraction of this reef is the large number of hard corals, primarily staghorn but also brain and uncommon cauliflower corals. As it's a shallow reef, you can see the coral polyps' unusual colourations of pinks, purples and blues.

The reef is also home to numerous fish. Clownfish in their anemone hosts, and plenty of morays which are really quite shy despite their fierce looks and those nasty teeth (which point backwards to prevent any morsels from escaping!). The reef teems with Picasso triggerfish, with their cream-coloured bodies streaked with orange and blue and a large black stripe through the eye area. They have small, toothy mouths and you will find them hunting and feeding on shrimps and sea urchins using their strong teeth.

The fish on this reef don't appear to receive too many visitors, and as a result some are very inquisitive and seem happy to pose for a few photos before dashing back into the corals.

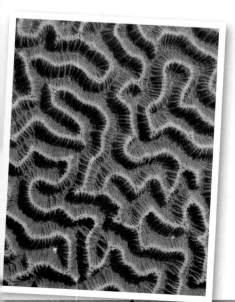

dard coral pattern ➚

Warning

When you go snorkelling, you need to keep your skin protected from the sun – because you're in the water you often don't realize you're burning until it's way too late. Wearing a T-shirt isn't enough: it will leave the backs of your legs exposed and sunburn behind your knees is particularly painful. You can wear a 0.5mm wetsuit or a shortie, or at the very least a rash vest. Whatever you choose, make sure you supplement it with plenty of sunblock, especially on your neck and on your ears.

East Coast

Murbah Reef

Slipper lobster

Ras Qidfa

A small and rocky headland that's full of hard corals and tiny, interesting critters.

Depth:	8m
Snorkelling:	Yes
Night dive:	Yes

GPS: N25°19'27.2" E56°22'56.0"

Distance from harbours:
Khor Fakkan Harbour 2.7nm
@ 204° (024°)
Lulaya Harbour 4.3nm
@ 201° (021°)

Leading into the bay towards Martini Rock, Ras Qidfa is a small, rocky headland where you'll find many hard corals and rocky boulders.

Diving

It's best to start your dive at the southern end of Ras Qidfa, and travel north towards Martini Rock bay, keeping the rocks, boulders and wall on your left-hand side. There's plenty to see here, including a multitude of fish species, turtles and hard and soft corals, although it becomes a little less interesting if you leave the rocky shores and venture onto the sandy seabed.

At night, simply follow the wall, keeping it on your left, and look in the nooks and crannies in the rocks for banded shrimp,

slipper lobsters and crayfish – it's an easy and pleasant spot for a dive after dark. There are not as many corals here as there are on other sites in the area, but you may be rewarded with glimpses of sleeping turtles, rays or even spotted eagle rays.

Shark Island

Port

Khor
Fakkan

10

20

Martini Rock

10

Ras Qidfa

N

Snorkelling

This is a good spot for snorkellers, especially if you enjoy the marine life on the seabed. It's a shallow site, and you will see most of the fish by staying close to the shoreline. If you venture further out you're probably only going to see moses sole, but then again, you might also be rewarded with the sight of rays or turtles.

Marine Life

There's plenty of fish life to see here; regularly spotted species include fusiliers, jacks and triggerfish. Look out for turtles and crayfish too.

If you search the featherstars carefully, you might find small shrimps and squat lobsters in them. These little critters camouflage themselves by changing their colours to match those of their hosts. There are also soft and hard corals that put on a show at night when they feed.

The Big Queasy

There are a number of tablets you can take for sea sickness, such as Dramamine, Stugeron and Dezinil. You may have to try them all out (on different dives, of course) to find which particular one suits you best. As with all medication, you need to be aware of the possible side-effects.

Some divers wear wrist bands with special pressure points on wrists or patches that look like mini plasters. Called Scopoderm, they are worn behind the ears, and these can be quite effective.

There are also other ways to minimise the chance of feeling seasick. When you're getting ready for a dive try to have all your gear lined up and placed within easy reach. This will enable you to kit up more quickly because the last thing you want is to be looking down for any length of time. While you're on the boat try and keep your eyes on the horizon.

If, after surfacing, you feel sick, take your equipment off and try get back into the water where you'll feel a lot better (if it's not rough, that is).

Make sure that you drink plenty of fluids before and after the dive to avoid becoming dehydrated.

squat lobster

Dive
59

Refinery Reef

An expansive coral site where you might spot some odd fish antics.

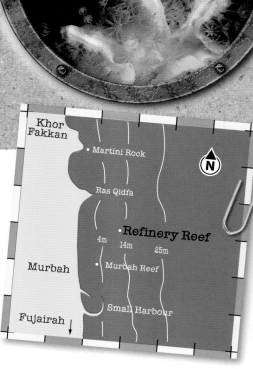
Solenocaulon coral

Depth:	28m
Snorkelling:	No
Night dive:	Yes
GPS:	N25°18'22.7" E56°23'10.9"

Distance from harbour:
FIMC 10.8nm. @ 8° (188°)

This is another of the reefs Scuba International located and it's very similar to Deep Reef (see p.98) in that the site consists of a sandy seabed with several slabs of plate corals, and other coral outcrops.

Diving

Going by boat, Refinery Reef is about 25 minutes or so from the Fujairah International Marine Club. It lies between 24 and 28m which means it's not a site for snorkellers. For divers though it offers a chance to see some varied corals and some interesting marine life.

Marine Life

This area is quite spread out, rather similar to Anemone and Coral Gardens in Khor Fakkan, and boasts all the usual types of corals - green whip corals and teddybear corals in shades of pink, orange and red.

There's also plenty of an unusual pretty yellow soft coral called *Solenocaulon*. *Solenocaulon* is covered with polyps on one side, and flat on the other.

If you approach slowly and look carefully, you can sometimes find small yellow gobies and squat lobsters hiding on the same coral. The lobsters will defend their territory from you by holding up their long

(Map labels: Khor Fakkan, Martini Rock, Ras Qidfa, N, Refinery Reef, 4m, 14m, 25m, Murbah, Murbah Reef, Small Harbour, Fujairah)

claws. You may also find a large and rather ugly flat fish called a turbot here. It looks very aggressive with its unusual eyes and many pointed teeth. If you get too close it will give you a start with the speed at which it swims out of your way.

Don't take the aggression too lightly: we were recently trying to photograph one on the seabed. As it didn't seem too phased by us, we tried to get closer for a picture of its amazing eyes. It began to swim away then appeared to have a change of heart and rapidly swam back and bit a diver on the arm. Luckily we were wearing wetsuits as it was winter and the diver got off with a few holes in the wetsuit and a bruised arm (and ego)!

Another unusual aspect of this site is the number of red tooth blue triggerfish that congregate here. During mating season, which is usually between June and August, these fish are fiercely territorial. If you attract their attention and they see you as a threat they'll charge at you, turning away only at the very last moment and just avoiding contact. Wearing blue fins seems to attract even more unwelcome attention from them. So time your dives so as not to coincide with summer if possible.

There's a jellyfish 'season' twice a year, usually from March to April and October to November. If you're diving here then take a close look as the jellyfish act as flying saucers, carrying all sorts of 'aliens' along in the current. Try and spot the juvenile fish, crabs and shrimps hiding in their tentacles – but be careful as most jellies have a nasty sting!

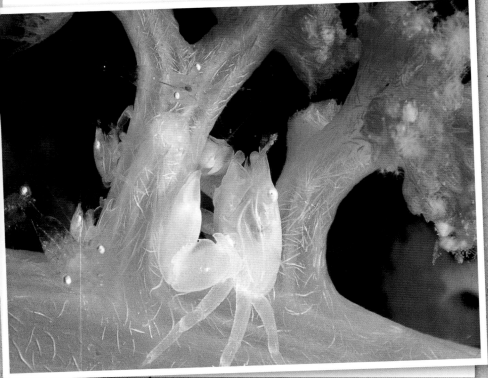

Porcelain squat lobster and shrimps

Shark Island

A great spot for chilling on the beach, diving, snorkelling and, yes, spotting a shark.

Other names: Khor Fakkan Island

Depth: 16m

Snorkelling: Yes

Night dive: Yes

GPS: N25°21'12.0" E56°22'36.2"

Distance from harbours:
Khor Fakkan Harbour 0.8nm @ 081° (261°)
Lulaya Harbour 2.5nm @ 183° (003°)

Distance from other dive site:
From Anemone Gardens (p.92) 0.2nm @ 318° (138°)
From Coral Gardens (p.96) 0.18nm @ 270° (90°)

This fairly large island stands proud at the south-eastern end of the magnificent Khor Fakkan bay. It has a great beach for picnicking on, to dive and snorkel from, or simply to spend a relaxing day in the sun.

Diving

The depth around the island varies: from a shallow 3-5m on the coastal side, it becomes deeper towards the seaward side. The bottom is sandy and rocky, with a variety of hard and soft corals. The island can be dived from its beach, but most divers are dropped off at either Coral Gardens or Anemone Gardens, and complete the latter part of the dive close to the island. Diving or swimming around the whole island is not possible in one dive.

On the south-west tip of the island is a site known as Shark Drift. This is best dived by starting at the deeper seaward-

Pufferfish

most point at 16m. Drift with the slight current and head around the island. This is an excellent and easy site to dive at night. There's usually lots of fish life to be found, including sleeping turtles in the rocky overhangs. You may also find large, tailless rays. These inquisitive creatures are wonderfully graceful, and look a bit like flying saucers from outer space. They're also often covered in several remoras that attach themselves with the sucker-disc on their head.

Be careful of discarded fishing nets, especially at night. If you do get tangled up in one, don't panic; stay still and signal to your buddy for help. The island is also covered with black urchins, that become active at night, so watch your buoyancy to avoid painful punctures!

Snorkelling

The snorkelling is sometimes better than the diving here, and the waters are shallow enough to be able to see the seabed from the surface. If you want to see sharks, stay at the south-western corner of the island.

During the winter months you're more likely to see blacktip reef sharks swimming in the shallow waters at 1-3m. You'll also find lots of hard and soft corals, turtles and rays if the visibility is good.

Marine Life

As the name suggests, this is a good place for sharks; particularly blacktip reef sharks that can be seen between November and April on the eastern point of the island.

On the seabed you may see cerianthid anemones, pretty purple or white fronds sticking out of a cardboard looking tube. Don't disturb or touch them as they'll retract down into their tubes.

This area is also the haunt of many schools of fish, from batfish and juvenile barracuda to big mouth mackerel, as well as pufferfish, large rays with remoras and the occasional spotted eagle ray in shallower water. During the winter months, you may sometimes see murex shells laying their straw-like eggs under the rocks.

Blacktip shark

Warning

The rocks around the island are covered with sea urchins and, at certain times of the year, with small brown swimming anemones that deliver a nasty sting if touched (see First Aid, p.159 for more information).

Dive 61

Sharm Rocks

Rich in marine life, this is a great site for leisurely sightseeing, particularly at night.

Other names: Three Rocks, Pinnacles, Rock Piles

Depth: 14m

Snorkelling: Yes

Night dive: Yes

GPS: N25°28'55.0" E56°21'57.1"

Distance from harbours:
Khor Fakkan Harbour 8.7nm @ 353° (173°)
Lulaya Harbour 5.3nm @ 348° (168°)

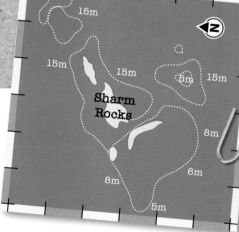

Not far from Snoopy Island and the Sandy Beach Motel are these four small outcrops of rock that just break the surface of the water at low tide. They are covered in masses of soft corals and there is a small table coral reef towards the shore in about 4m of water.

Note that navigation can be difficult here as the small sandy gullies or alleys can be misleading and disorientating. The former owner of Sandy Beach Dive Centre placed two mooring buoys on the north side of the rocks, close to the deepest part of the site. Their upkeep has been continued by the staff of Sandy Beach Motel. It's a good idea to make use of these buoys, rather than throwing in your anchor and damaging the reef.

Diving

It is possible to complete a circuit of these rocks in one dive, but it can be a rush, even in 60 minutes. The seaward side of the rocks consists of a vertical rocky wall that goes down to 14m, while the shore side has a shallow table coral reef to one side and boulder coral outcrops on the other. This is another excellent shallow site for night dives, but take your time, as it's crammed with marine life. Peer into the corals for fish seeking protection from the night hunters. You will find lots of sleeping parrotfish, broomtailed wrasse and sometimes sleeping turtles.

If you look hard, you may find a piece of moving coral attached to a sandy, dusty looking crab. This is a decorator crab and there are many different species here. The crab steals pieces of coral polyps from the main coral colony and attaches them to its own body for camouflage – incredible!

Snorkelling

The variety of fish life makes Sharm Rocks a very special location for snorkellers, and for some reason the parrotfish, boxfish and broomtailed wrasse appear to be larger here than elsewhere. All these fish are visible when snorkelling and you may also see rays and turtles. If you're a strong swimmer, you can swim out to the rocks from the mainland in about 10 minutes (depending on the weather), but hire a boat if you tire easily.

Marine Life

These rocks are full of shoals of fish; jacks, big mouth mackerel, fusiliers and

Construction Halts Play

While the construction work on the East Coast Island promises new habitats for some exciting marine life, it has also involved huge quantities of sand being dredged up from the seabed and transported to the island. As a result, some of the sites have been damaged or covered in silt, and visibility has been dramatically reduced. We would strongly recommend that you wait until construction work has been completed before diving a site near the island. Check in with the local dive centres to find out whether a site is good to dive again.

sometimes squid. You may also see turtles, morays, crayfish and guitar sharks. Explore the bottom for moses soles – their mottled scales provide excellent camouflage against the seabed. All that gives them away is the tiny gold flecks on their bodies. In early evening at the beginning of the warmer months, you can see the strange and beautiful mating habits of boxfish and cuttlefish. At the same time, look out for the small, but fierce, clownfish defending their anemone host, which hides and protects their brood of eggs.

Snoopy Island

Marine life on your doorstep! It doesn't get much more accessible than this.

Juvenile lionfish

Other names: Jazirat Al Gubbah

Depth: 8m

Snorkelling: Yes

Night dive: Yes

GPS: N25°29'29.0" E56°21'59.0"

Distance from harbours:
Khor Fakkan Harbour 8nm @ 359° (179°)
Lulaya Harbour 5.5nm @ 350° (170°)

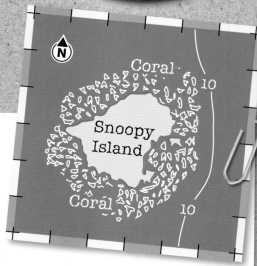

Named because it's shaped like Snoopy lying on his back with his nose in the air, the slopes of this small island are covered by several varieties of hard coral that are home to a wealth of anemones and clownfish.

At high tide, it's a good 10 minute swim to the edge of the island. However, during November there are unusually high and low tides that make it possible to walk to the island without getting wet!

Snoopy Island can be visited from Sandy Beach Motel, which has a dive operator whose facilities you can use and who you can hire equipment from. If you don't hire eqiupment and have non-divers with you, there is a beach entrance fee of around

Dhs.40. In an attempt to protect its guests, the motel prohibits anyone from using boats and jet skis around the island. However, boats still occasionally pass between the island and the shore, so take care.

Diving

Snoopy Island is the only shore dive on the East Coast, making it one of the easiest (and most affordable) dives, seeing as you don't

have to rely on a dive operator. Put your fins on in waist-high water then swim out a little before descending.

The southern side of the island offers the more interesting diving. There's plenty to see here, including varied and plentiful marine life and several species of hard and soft corals and anemones.

On a night dive, the trip from the shore to the island is very interesting; look out for sleeping fish, as well as starfish, sand dollars, crabs and molluscs, all busy looking for their evening meal. You'll also see shrimps, but only because their eyes shine out from the sand. Try turning your torch off for a moment and seeing how many shrimp you can spot.

When you arrive at the rocks and corals at the base of the island, we suggest you turn right, keeping the island on your left. You'll encounter sleeping fish, morays and the occasional barracuda. There are also a few anemones with sleeping clownfish. Sometimes the anemones completely close up, resembling a big, blue plastic bag. We were almost chased out of the water by a lionfish on a night

dive here when we persisted in taking too many photos of it.

Snorkelling

Snoopy Island is the most accessible East Coast location for snorkellers and is relatively protected from all weather, except exceptionally heavy seas. The site is popular and on weekends can be rather busy. But it's also a very shallow site, so you'll be able to see plenty of marine life. Snorkellers are often more likely than divers to encounter the guitar and blacktip sharks that appear in the cooler months.

Marine Life

There's a lot of marine life to see, although there's less coral on the shore side than on the seaward side. You can expect to see big mouth mackerel, morays, anemones, clownfish and lionfish. You may also see turtles and sharks. Look out for smaller marine life; pipefish, shrimps, crabs, and nudibranchs, too.

Tiger shrimp ↗

Further Information

Natural World

Marine life in the region's waters is varied and plentiful. Below are some of the creatures that divers, snorkellers and beach lovers will be thrilled to see.

Marine Life

The shallow warm waters here allow for reefs that teem with fish, while dugongs graze on sea grass beds and turtles come ashore to lay their eggs. For more detailed information on the region's marine life, check out the books listed in the Bibliography on p.179.

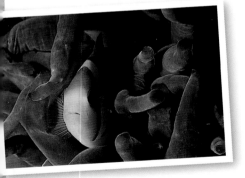

Clownfish
Several species of this lovely patterned fish are common residents of coral reefs, where they live among the arms of the sea anemone. While the sea anemone's sting kills other fish, the clownfish is immune to the poison and feeds on the host's leftovers.

Bottle-nosed Dolphin
Tursiops truncatus

This is the largest of the eight species of dolphin that have been recorded in UAE waters. They are often encountered on east coast boat trips, when they come to play around the boat and show off their incredible acrobatic skills. Other dolphins that live here are the common, the spinner and the humpback dolphin. Whales are also represented in this region by four species of toothed whales, as well as the enormous sperm whale.

Blacktip Reef Shark
There are at least 10 species of sharks in UAE waters, including reef, blacktip,

hammerheads and tiger sharks. Very few of the potentially dangerous sharks come in close enough to shore to present a problem to swimmers. The pearl divers of old considered themselves to be more at risk from an attack by barracuda than from sharks.

Paper Nautilus
Argonauta hians

This extraordinary shell can be found on the beaches of the Arabian Gulf during February and March. The beautiful, feather-light structure is made by the argonaut octopus and held underneath her belly after she's deposited her eggs in it. Baby octopuses have a protected environment until the mother lets them go and their cradle washes up on the beach.

Sundial Shell
Architectonica perspectiva

The east coast beaches have different shells to those of the Arabian Gulf coast. The sundial shell can be found on Kalba beach, while further north is a good place to find the opercula (plate-like structures that close the opening of a shell when the organism is retracted) of a sea snail.

Manta Ray

Like sharks, rays are cartilaginous fish, which means that their skeleton is made of a tough, elastic substance rather than bone. There are many different kinds of rays – manta, eagle, bull and marble rays are just a few types seen off the Gulf coast.

Most rays feed on crustaceans, molluscs, oysters and are bottom dwellers. Some, like the manta ray, prefer open water and feed on plankton. While the stingray does inflict an excruciatingly painful sting, all the other rays are harmless and none are aggressive. The stingray tends to bury itself in sand in shallow water and may be inadvertently stepped on by bathers. If you shuffle your feet as you wade in, you'll find the stingrays will hastily swim off at your approach.

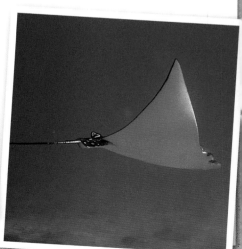

Sea Cow or Dugong
Dugong dugon

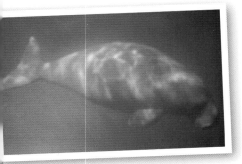

Although it's highly unlikely that you will ever see this marine mammal, it deserves a mention because of its history and future. It is the animal that gave rise to the legend of the mermaid. Related to elephants and rock hyrax, it has breasts between its front legs, nails instead of claws and lives in herds led by a female. There are probably less than a thousand of these gentle creatures left in the Gulf, where they face the continual hazards of shipping, oil pollution and degradation of the sea grasses that they feed on. The Arabic name 'arus al bahr' means 'bride of the sea'.

Green Turtle
Chelonia mydas

A few decades ago green turtles used to haul themselves up onto Dubai beaches by the dozens to lay their eggs. Now their nesting grounds are covered by harbours, hotels and high rises and their breeding sites are restricted to some of the offshore islands. Although five species of sea turtle have been recorded in the region, only the green turtle and the hawksbill turtle breed here. The breeding season is in the early summer (May – August).

Marine Life Table

Cephalopods	West Coast	Musandam	East Coast
Cuttlefish	✓	✓	✓
Octopus		✓	✓
Squid		✓	✓
Corals (Hard)			
Black	✓	✓	✓
Boulder		✓	✓
Brain	✓	✓	✓
Daisy		✓	✓
Favite	✓	✓	✓
Leaf		✓	✓
Lettuce		✓	✓

Corals (Hard)	West Coast	Musandam	East Coast
Pavona/leaf			✓
Porities	✓	✓	✓
Staghorn	✓	✓	✓
Table		✓	✓
Coral (Soft)			
Anemone	✓	✓	✓
Cerianthid			✓
Cauliflower coral	✓	✓	✓
Cave coral	✓	✓	✓
Dandelion coral		✓	✓
Hydrocoral/sea fir	✓	✓	✓

Coral (Soft)	West Coast	Musandam	East Coast
Octocoral	✓	✓	✓
Purple		✓	✓
Seafan		✓	✓
Sea pen	✓	✓	✓
Teddybear		✓	✓
Whip	✓	✓	✓
Crustaceans			
Cigalle	✓	✓	✓
Crab	✓	✓	✓
Crayfish		✓	✓
Cleaner shrimp	✓	✓	✓
Decorator crab		✓	✓
Hermit crab	✓	✓	✓
Shrimp	✓	✓	✓
Slipper lobster	✓	✓	✓
Spiny lobster	✓	✓	✓
Echinoderms			
Crinoid/feather star	✓	✓	✓
Crown of thorns	✓	✓	✓
Sand dollar	✓	✓	✓
Sea urchin	✓	✓	✓
Starfish	✓	✓	✓
Fish			
Three bar bream	✓	✓	✓
Angelfish	✓	✓	✓
Anthias		✓	✓
Barracuda	✓	✓	✓
Batfish	✓	✓	✓
Blenny	✓	✓	✓
Boxfish	✓	✓	✓
Broomtailed wrasse		✓	✓
Butterflyfish		✓	✓
Cardinalfish		✓	✓

Fish	West Coast	Musandam	East Coast
Catfish		✓	✓
Citron goby			✓
Clownfish	✓	✓	✓
Conger eel			✓
Cornetfish		✓	✓
Crocodilefish			✓
Cowfish		✓	
Damselfish	✓	✓	✓
Diamond trevally	✓		
Dottyback	✓	✓	✓
Emperor/angelfish		✓	✓
Flounder		✓	✓
Frogfish		✓	✓
Fusilier	✓	✓	✓
Goatfish	✓	✓	✓
Goby	✓	✓	✓
Grouper	✓	✓	✓
Halibut			✓
Hammour	✓	✓	✓
Hawkfish		✓	✓
Honeycomb morays		✓	✓
Jawfish (hole goby)		✓	✓
Jack/tuna	✓	✓	✓
Kingfish	✓	✓	✓
Lionfish	✓	✓	✓
Mackerel	✓	✓	✓
Moses sole		✓	✓
Moray eel	✓	✓	✓
Mullet		✓	✓
Oceanic triggerfish	✓		
Parrotfish	✓	✓	✓
Pennantfish	✓	✓	✓
Picasso triggerfish			✓

Fish	West Coast	Musandam	East Coast
Pipefish	✓	✓	✓
Pufferfish	✓	✓	✓
Pygmy seamoth			✓
Queenfish		✓	✓
Rabbitfish	✓		
Razorfish/shrimpfish			✓
Red big-eye			✓
Remora	✓	✓	✓
Robust pipefish			✓
Sergeant major	✓	✓	✓
Scorpionfish	✓	✓	✓
Seahorse			✓
Snapper	✓	✓	✓
Sohal	✓	✓	✓
Soldierfish		✓	✓
Squirrelfish	✓	✓	✓
Stonefish	✓		
Striped eel catfish			✓
Sunfish		✓	
Surgeonfish	✓	✓	✓
Sweetlips	✓	✓	✓
Tobyfish			✓
Trevally	✓	✓	✓

Other	West Coast	Musandam	East Coast
Algae	✓	✓	✓
Dolphin	✓	✓	✓
Jellyfish	✓	✓	✓
Sea snake	✓		
Sea squirt	✓	✓	✓
Turtle	✓	✓	✓

Rays	West Coast	Musandam	East Coast
Bell	✓	✓	✓
Eagle	✓	✓	✓
Electric/torpedo	✓	✓	✓
Feather-tailed	✓	✓	✓
Guitar/shovelnose	✓	✓	✓
Leopard	✓		
Manta/devil		✓	✓
Marble	✓		✓
Stingray	✓	✓	✓

Sharks	West Coast	Musandam	East Coast
Blacktip reef		✓	✓
Blind juvenile	✓	✓	
Bull		✓	
Grey reef		✓	
Hammerhead		✓	✓
Leopard	✓	✓	
Nurse		✓	
Shark eggs		✓	
Whaleshark	✓	✓	
Whitetip		✓	
Zebra		✓	✓

Shells & Worms	West Coast	Musandam	East Coast
Barnacle	✓	✓	✓
Cone shell	✓	✓	✓
Cowrie shell	✓	✓	✓
Encrusting worm	✓	✓	✓
Fanworm	✓	✓	✓
Featherworm	✓	✓	✓
Flatworm	✓	✓	✓
Murex shell	✓	✓	✓
Nudibranch	✓	✓	✓
Pearl oyster	✓	✓	✓
Sea hare	✓	✓	✓
Thorny oyster shell	✓	✓	✓

Sponges	West Coast	Musandam	East Coast
Sponges	✓	✓	✓

Environment and the Law

The UAE's need and enthusiasm for developments that outdo each other in the use of superlatives is understandable. The problem of course, is the conflict between this drive and the need to conserve the country's natural resources.

At the Environment 2001 Conference and Exhibition in Abu Dhabi, the UAE committed itself to investing US$46 billion on projects related to the environment over the next 10 years.

The UAE is also party to international agreements on biodiversity, climate change, desertification, endangered species, hazardous wastes, marine dumping and ozone layer protection. In addition to country-wide environmental controls, in 2001 the Dubai government banned any further development along the coast without prior permission, although that seems something of a paradox in light of the construction projects that have been authorised to go ahead.

Despite the efforts being made, there are some serious environmental issues facing the UAE. The massive scale of development being pursued in Dubai on gigantic projects such as the three Palm Islands, the World and Dubai Waterfront, will change the coastline of Dubai and its ecosystem immeasurably (see 'Life Under The Palms' on p.22).

Conservationists have suggested that the massive construction in the Arabian Gulf could be damaging breeding grounds for the endangered hawksbill turtle, as well as destroying coral reefs and fish stocks. The developers, however, argue that the sites will attract sealife, and point to the recent increases in fish and marine life witnessed around the crescent on the Palm Jumeirah.

Many conservationists slate the rapid expansion of Dubai's infrastructure, however the whole issue is something of a double-edged sword. Many other countries enjoyed their boom-time in the early part of the last century, when environmental issues were not as prominent as they are today, so in some ways it seems unfair that the UAE shouldn't be allowed to develop as other nations have. Then again, the UAE has the advantage of being able to learn from experience – if there had been more environmental awareness during the industrialisation of leading nations, perhaps the world would currently be in a better position. Whatever side you are on, it's not unreasonable to say that there are some environmental issues that could, and should, be given more consideration.

The Federal Law for Environmental Development and Protection provides for the use, protection and development of water resources. The law regulates fishing and navigation activities in ways that are intended to protect marine life and water resources in the UAE.

Marine Protected Areas

According to the UAE's Federal Environmental Agency, the UAE has 14 protected areas, covering a total of 4,446km². The marine PAs among these include Marawah and Al Wathba Wetland in Abu Dhabi, Jazirat Sir Bu Na'air in Sharjah and Al Aqqa, Al Faqit and Dhadnah in Fujairah.

In all of these areas fishing and coral or shell collecting is prohibited. However, although there are signs on the beaches to indicate that these areas are protected and that certain activities are prohibited, the rules often appear to be ignored – whether this is due to a lack of awareness or enforcement isn't certain.

When addressing a symposium on protected areas in January 2000, the managing director of Abu Dhabi's Environmental Research and Wildlife Development Agency (ERWDA) was frank in admitting that while many areas have been afforded protection through legislation, the protection has rarely been carefully planned or properly implemented. The result is that environmental goals that have been set, have rarely been met.

The Marawah Marine Protected Area in Abu Dhabi is one of the largest such areas in the Gulf. Its sea grass beds, dugongs and turtles make it a particularly important resource.

Dugongs and Turtles

Dugongs, hawksbill and green turtles make up some of the UAE's most ecologically important, and endangered, marine species. Dugongs are listed as vulnerable to extinction, while hawksbill turtles are listed as critically endangered and green turtles as endangered.

	Hawksbill Turtle	Green Turtle
Colour:	Dark, greenish-brown	Brown (despite the name). Juveniles are almost black when they hatch but lighten in colour
Length:	55-95cm	80-120cm
Weight:	About 55kg	130-250kg
Habitat:	Reefs and rocky areas	Inlets and bays
Diet:	Sea urchins, sponges, molluscs and sea squirts	The young turtles feed on creatures like jellyfish and shellfish. The adults feed on sea grass and algae
Status:	Critically endangered	Endangered
Identifying features :	Narrow upper jaw with a distinctive overbite. Two claws on each front flipper. The scales (or scutes) on their shells overlap	Serrated jaw. One claw on each front flipper

under threat. Gill net fishing, especially the use of drift nets, is said to be the main cause of death among the UAE's dugongs. The second biggest threat to a dugong is being hit by a boat.

Dugongs and turtles are also threatened by the damage that's being done to their habitats and breeding grounds through coastal development, dredging and pollution. When turtles come ashore to lay their eggs, they are easily disturbed by people and vehicle movement, and their nests are vulnerable to predation by people and feral dogs.

The Arabian Gulf and Red Sea are said to be home to a population of over 5,000 dugongs, making it the largest population of these creatures outside of Australia. Of these, about 40% are found in the waters off the UAE, specifically off Abu Dhabi.

While dugongs and turtles are protected under federal law, they are constantly

Did You Know?

- 60% of marine rubbish consists of plastic – bags, sweet wrappers, bottles, straws and the like
- Cigarette butts have been found in the stomachs of fish, whales and turtles
- It takes more than 12 years for a cigarette butt to disintegrate

Environmental Action

It may not seem like it, but every diver can make a difference to the environment – both bad and good. Here are some ways to create a positive impact.

If you feel strongly about the environment, why not do something about it? You can contact one of the environmental groups in the UAE – they always need volunteers and funds. Playing an active role in protecting the underwater environment will also increase the pleasure you get from diving.

Emirates Diving Association

The Emirates Diving Association is a non-profit organisation, accredited by the United Nations Environment Programme, that consists of a handful of volunteers who share a passion for the marine environment. They have signed a memorandum of understanding with the UAE Ministry of Environment and Water to protect the UAE's shoreline and reefs. EDA also actively drives various conservation projects such as a reef

monitoring programme and clean-ups
of dive sites and they arrange dive trips.
Contact them on 04 393 9390 or visit
www.emiratesdiving.com.

Emirates Environmental Group

This is a voluntary, non-governmental
organisation devoted to protecting
the environment in general through
education, action programmes
and community involvement.
Activities include evening lectures
on environmental topics, recycling
collections and clean-up campaigns.
Annual membership costs Dhs.50 for
adults and Dhs.20-30 for students.
Contact them on 04 331 8100 or visit
www.eeg-uae.org.

← Martini Bay Beach

Eco-diving Practices

On an individual level, every diver can do their bit towards protecting
or preserving the marine environment.

- Don't remove any creatures – even if they appear to be dead.

- Don't 'ride' turtles – they will panic and drown.

- Don't touch any marine creature: they could be harmful, they could
  be harmed and they will certainly be scared off. It's far more
  satisfying to observe them going about their daily routines.

- Don't touch corals. Hard corals are made up of millions of
  zooxanthellae which they need to grow and to form the foundation
  of their limestone skeleton. Soft corals consist of delicate polyps.
  If you touch them, you'll kill them. In addition, coral cuts are
  notoriously likely to become infected and take a long time to heal.

- Don't litter or dump rubbish.

- When you're out on a dive, do your fellow divers and the marine
  environment a favour and collect any litter you find. Empty plastic
  bags, cans, old bottles and discarded fishing nets can kill marine
  life (but check that there aren't any creatures inside them before
  removing them from the site).

- Maintain your buoyancy – this means you're less likely to crash into
  any delicate corals.

- Take care when anchoring.

- If you have a picnic on the beach, throw your rubbish away in the
  bins provided or, better still, take it away with you.

Diving

A couple of things are really important to divers: their training, gear, health... and a good insurance policy.
And once all the basics are in place, you can then start to broaden your underwater horizons.

Training

Most people are curious about the underwater world, but they're also understandably nervous about the idea of breathing underwater. Fortunately, most courses are well-structured and easy-to-follow and will take you from apprehensive to advanced in no time.

In order to be able to dive anywhere in the world, you must complete, and pass, an open water diver course from any one of the reputable training organisations – CMAS, NAUI, PADI, SSI and SDI. (Of these, PADI is the largest, and the one you're most likely to encounter.) As proof of this, you'll receive a certification card (a 'C-card') which allows you to go on an 'open water' rated dive of up to 18m in depth.

A good dive school will then encourage you to go on a few pleasure dives with an instructor: this will help you to build confidence and apply the skills you've learnt. The aim is to make those skills a reflex action so you feel comfortable enough in the water to start

wondering about what's next. (For a list of schools, see the Dive Directory on p.181.)

What's next is advanced diver training. A dive agency generally packages a few courses that focus on specific skills together. (See the tip box opposite to see what a PADI advanced programme consists of. Other dive agencies will offer something similar.) This is a good way for you to upgrade your skills and explore aspects of diving that are of particular interest to you, but there's no real industry standard as to what makes an advanced diver.

What About The Kids?
There are various underwater programmes designed for children. These familiarise kids with the underwater environment, teach them water skills and prepare them for scuba diving.

Neptune Diving in Dubai is planning on introducing diving to school pupils as an extra-curricular activity, and arranging summer dive camps. For contact details see the Dive Directory on p.181

Basically your advanced course will end with you feeling well-versed in many of the less exciting, but nevertheless important aspects of diving, such as dive planning, navigation, using a dive computer, boat dives, dealing with currents and safety procedures. You'll also have an opportunity to do more of the stuff that really interests you, be it diving on wrecks, diving at night or learning more about the life you'll see down there.

Once you've got an advanced diver certification, you'll find there is still plenty more to do. It's a good idea to complete a rescue and first aid course, for example. And then, if this is where your interests lie, you'll be ready to take on the more technical side of diving, such as diving on Nitrox and going to depths of 30 to 40m, which is the generally accepted recreational diving limit.

Technical Diving

Diving becomes technical when you go beyond the recreational diving limit of 40m. In technical diving you use mixed gases to increase your bottom time or, in extreme technical diving, replace them with inert gases to lower the risks.

As it might suggest, technical diving involves far more complicated equipment, which is a sizeable investment. Dive planning also takes on a whole new meaning, and you're going to have to be a lot more committed to the sport than a recreational diver. Your fitness becomes more important as you deal with increased time in the water and the weight of your gear. In other words, technical diving takes you way beyond recreational diving. It's not for everyone, but for enthusiasts the ability to reach new depths is exhilarating.

For more information on this type of diving, contact British Sub Aqua Club, Scuba International or Technical Diving International Center, (details in the Dive Directory on p.181).

A PADI Advanced Open Water Programme

PADI offers the following 'Adventures in Diving' programme, but most agencies offer a similar set of options, prerequisites and qualifications.

What do you need?
Open water diver or qualifying certification from PADI or any other recognised organisation. You have to be at least 15 years old (or 12 for the PADI Junior Advanced Open Water Diver).

What does the course involve?
The course includes deep diving, underwater navigation and a choice of three from the following: Altitude Diver, Boat Diver, Deep Diver, Diver Propulsion Vehicle, Drift Diver, Dry Suit Diver, Multilevel Diver, Night Diver, Peak Performance Buoyancy, Search and Recovery Diver, Underwater Naturalist, Underwater Navigator, Underwater Photographer, Underwater Videographer, AWARE Fish Identification or Wreck Diver.

The course requires at least 15 hours of lessons and you'll complete a minimum of five dives over two days.

Then what?
You can now sign up for dives that require your new set of skills, and you can enroll in further specialty courses such as rescue, deep or wreck diving or underwater photography (see opposite).

Equipment

With diving being such a popular sport in the UAE, dive gear is easy to find and the range is generally good. For a full list of dive gear suppliers, see the Dive Directory on p.181.

Entry-level dive gear or snorkelling kits are generally widely available in the UAE. Go Sports, for example, stock a range of Mares and Cressi gear from fins and masks to regulators and dive computers. You'll find a range of wetsuits there – even semi-dry suits! – and some good dive bags.

Al Boom Marine and Scuba Dubai in Dubai and Gulf Marine Sports and Mohammed Bin

Masaood & Sons in Abu Dhabi are best for your higher-end, more specialised gear. Staff will be able to advise you on your purchases and they do airfills and service your gear too.

Many of your dives here will be done as part of a group and you'll go out to the site by boat. Seeing as most dive gear is pretty uniform (black neoprene with possibly a splash of colour), it makes sense to mark your gear so that you'll be able to spot it quickly on a dive boat or in a dive centre when everyone is kitting up.

Rinsing your gear off well in cold, desalinated water after each dive is a must and the climate requires that you need to do gear maintenance checks more frequently than you might elsewhere in the world.

Suiting Up for Gulf Diving

While Gulf waters are typically warm, every diver has different tolerance levels for the

Temp.	Protection
30°C+	Lycra or 0.5mm suit for protection from the sun, hydrocorals and jellyfish
26-29°C	0.5mm suit or 2.5mm shortie wetsuit for a little protection
23-25°C	3mm one or two piece suit consisting of farmer john and jacket
18-22°C	5mm one or two piece suit consisting of farmer john and jacket
18°C	5 or 7mm semi- or dry suit

Breathe Right

If you haven't been diving in a while, it's a really good idea to have your regulator serviced before you get back into the water. Also, always take care to rinse your reg thoroughly after a dive and make sure that you put the dust cap on once you've disconnected it from the cylinder.

cold and you'll feel even chillier if you're doing repetitive dives, long dives or deep dives. How thick you want your wetsuit to be also depends on the time of year you're going diving (see the Water Temperatures table below). If you get cold easily or are doing a deep dive, wearing a hood could be your best bet. When you consider that up to 30% of your body heat is lost through your head, it's not surprising to find that a hood makes a huge difference. The chart opposite provides some guidelines to help you choose what degree of protection you will need.

Heavy Metal

European rules state that a visual inspection of your cylinder, whether it's a stainless steel or aluminium one, is required every two-and-a-half years. In the Gulf however, due to the heat, humidity and high salinity, it's recommended that your cylinders receive a visual inspection once a year, and that they are hydro-tested every five years.

Water Temperatures

Alongside is a table of monthly average water temperatures, given in Celsius, for the southern Arabian Gulf, the east coast and Musandam. However, note that temperatures are often affected by unpredictable thermoclines that result from cold water flowing in from the Indian Ocean.

Months	Arabian Gulf	East Coast & Musandam
January	18 - 23	21 - 23
February	20 - 23	20 - 23
March	20 - 25	20 - 24
April	24 - 26	22 - 24
May	27 - 30	22 - 27
June	27 - 32	23 - 27
July	31 - 35	28 - 30
August	33 - 36	32 - 30
September	30 - 33	31 - 29
October	30 - 33	30 - 27
November	25 - 30	29 - 26
December	23 - 25	26 - 23

Underwater Photography

Once you're diving, the next natural impulse is to record your underwater sightings – even if only to show landlubbers how exciting your sport is!

Underwater photography is becoming increasingly accessible thanks to the advent of digital cameras (which are less expensive than SLR or film cameras), and the growing availability of underwater housings.

Of course as soon as you head underwater colour is lost. The light spectrum is absorbed by water, starting with the reds and oranges and followed by yellows and greens. You'll need to bring out the colour of the reef life by using a strobe. This will allow the true beauty of the underwater realm to dazzle.

Composition is also important. You'll need to fill the frame as much as possible with your subject, which means getting as close to it as you can. To add to the challenge you also generally need to try and shoot your subject from below rather than above – camouflage is how most creatures under the water make it to old age, but it also greatly increases the difficulties an underwater photographer faces. Many wide-angle images don't look like much to anyone, even the most enthusiastic diver, without a human subject in them. A hole in a wreck isn't all that exciting. Frame your dive buddy in that hole to show how big or small it is and suddenly your shot has a whole lot more impact.

Your dive buddy is an essential part of your photographic expedition for reasons other than a close-at-hand model. They can help you position your strobe to best effect, keep an eye on you and remind you of your dive profile, depth, time and air when you're likely to be caught up in the excitement of taking photographs.

Cameras and Housings

There are two options when it comes to buying cameras and housings. You can either choose an all-in-one system of an amphibious camera complete with interchangeable lenses, a choice of strobes and other accessories. These, like the Sea&Sea MX10, Motormarine II or Nikonos V, are excellent choices for beginners. Alternatively, you could use a standard camera housed in a watertight case. You then still need to buy a port and gears for the lens, plus a strobe or two. And you have to hope that housing never ever springs a leak. A digital camera and underwater housing costs around Dhs.2,500 and a JVC video camera and marine pack housing will cost about Dhs.5,000.

Photography Checklist

- Use the camera on land several times to familiarise yourself with it
- Select the appropriate housing according to camera model, cost and so forth
- Always check that the batteries are fully charged
- Check all camera settings prior to your dive
- If using an additional strobe, check the batteries and the connection
- Leak test the housing in a 'dunk pool' prior to entering the sea
- Select a dive site you know well so you have an idea of what underwater subjects are available
- Get close to your subject – the less distance between the lens and subject, the better
- Observe your subject for a few moments before you take the photograph
- Fill the frame with your subject
- If possible look at the results and consider how you can improve on them before taking the next photograph
- If you're able to change the settings (known as bracketing) do so and take more photographs of the same subject
- Always rinse the camera and housing in fresh water after the dive
- Ensure the camera is completely dry before opening the housing and downloading the results or removing the film
- Remember to reload fresh batteries, insert the memory card and regrease the o-rings as necessary

You can also rent an underwater camera for about Dhs.250 per day or a video camera for around Dhs.350 per day from most of the dive centres.

Photographic Courses

If you've never used a digital camera, or used a camera underwater, you might want to consider some lessons.

The PADI Digital Underwater Photography and Videographer specialties are available to snorkellers and certified divers at most of the PADI dive centres (see Dive Directory on p.181). They cover the basics of the equipment you need to use, camera preparation, photographic techniques, colour, composition, resolution settings and downloading images. The photographer course costs about Dhs.800 – 1,200 and the videographer course is about Dhs.1,200 – 2,000. The courses include two sea dives, use of camera equipment, computer equipment and burning a CD of your first images. Costs will depend on whether you have your own equipment or use the dive centre's gear, which is recommended initially.

Where you shop in Dubai depends on what you want to buy. Canon have their headquarters in Bur Dubai and Sony brand equipment is available from Jumbo. Sea&Sea is available at Al Boom Marine. Ikelite and Subal are specialist housing systems and they are available for most of the high-end point and shoot as well as SLR camera brands, such as Nikon, Canon, Olympus, Sony, Fuji and Kodak. Underwater housings are often as expensive as the cameras themselves and range from Dhs.700 to Dhs.14,000 and upwards. Scuba Dubai stocks a good range.

Fitness and Insurance

When you head down under you want to know you've got an insurance policy that covers you, the number of the nearest diving doctor and a hotline to a recompression chamber - just in case.

Before you can sign up for a course, your dive school will request that you complete a form regarding your general health. If you reply yes to any of the questions on it, you will be required to obtain a certificate from a doctor stating that you're fit enough to dive and that you don't have any conditions, such as asthma or epilepsy, that would prevent you from diving.

During your course - and subsequent ones - diving safety, fitness and first aid will be taught. However, things can still go wrong.

Most general insurance polices don't cover diving - and not all companies will cover sports diving even if you specifically ask for this to be included. So whether it's travel or personal insurance you're after, you need to be aware that sport diving is in a category of its own. If you dive regularly you may find an annual insurance policy value for money. Remember to check if there is a limit on the number or length of the trips you can take, if there's any excess to be paid in the event of a claim and whether there's a limit on the depth, number or types of dives you can do.

A policy should cover the following: cancellation of a trip, missed or delayed departure, loss of personal documents and money, loss of personal property (check if there's a limit on the value of single items), diving equipment, personal accident, medical cover, hospital benefits, personal liability, legal expenses and assistance and hyperbaric treatment.

Emergency Contact Numbers
Dubai Police
Rescue Department 999

West Coast:
EXOMOS 04 883 5222.

East Coast:
Scuba International 09 222 0060

Diving Physicians

Horst Käfer, Dr Akel's Clinic,
04 344 2773, 050 652 3809

Suliman Nayal, Polyclinic,
Port Saeed, 04 295 9444

Jamal Ali Jammal, Dubai
Physiotherapy Clinic, 04 349 6333

Why Diving And Dentists
Go Together

Why Diving And Dentists Go Together

Regular visits to the dentist should be high on a diver's agenda. There are three main problems divers can encounter: muscle or joint pain, tooth squeeze and pain caused by ill-fitting dentures. If you've just visited a dentist and have a temporary filling, make sure you tell him that you're planning to dive and ask if the filling will be OK to dive. That way it won't be only the sharks down there with a toothy grin.

Divers Alert Network (DAN) is a non-profit medical and research organisation that provides medical information, diving insurance and emergency assistance.

Recompression Chambers

Scuba International (09 222 0060) in Fujairah has a recompression chamber that's available 24 hours a day with operators on call, and they have linked up with the Fujairah Coast Guard to provide emergency assistance to commercial and sport divers throughout the UAE. In summer 2006 the dive centre was in the process of moving their recompression chamber to the Fujairah Port Clinic.

In July 2006 EXOMOS (04 883 5222), a submersibles company, was installing a recompression chamber in Jebel Ali which was expected to be commissioned, and available for public use, before the end of 2006. They would then move the chamber to their new offices at the Dubai Port Company by the end of 2007.

DAN is familiar to most divers – which isn't surprising considering it's the largest global diver organisation. DAN membership entitles you to 24 hour medical assistance in the event of a medical emergency, worldwide. This means that if you find yourself in trouble, DAN will organise medical transport, coordinate hyperbaric and medical treatment, refer you to medical specialists and assist with travel arrangements for you or a family member.

Insurance through DAN is specific to diving, valid worldwide and there are no excess fees. They also cover your travel and dive gear. And seeing as you hopefully may not ever need DAN's assistance, you'll still receive benefits in the form of a subscription to their magazine, special offers and access to seminars and conferences on underwater safety.

A basic membership costs €68 (about Dhs.318) and this covers unlimited medical transportation, the cost of hospitalisation, hyberbaric therapy, medical costs for emergency treatment of a diving injury, repatriation costs and the expenses incurred if you have to stay in another country for a

Fit To Dive

If you've had surgery, it's imperative that you are fully healed and that your strength, general fitness and well-being is back to normal before you dive again. Before you do dive again, make sure your doctor is aware of your intentions and that you take heed of any advice or recommendations they might make.

longer time than you'd intended, as a result of an underwater accident. There are a number of plans available, including options for diving professionals.

The DAN network consists of five independent, non-profit organisations (DAN America, DAN Europe, DAN Southern Africa, DAN Japan, DAN South East Asia Pacific) that are funded by their members' fees. The UAE and the rest of the Gulf falls under DAN Europe.

The Professional Association of Diving Instructions (PADI) also provides comprehensive dive insurance through Vicencia & Buckley. However, if you live outside the US this policy is only available to PADI professional members and members of the PADI Diving Society.

Cover includes medical treatment for everything diving related (from ear injuries to decompression sickness), medical and rescue expenses, loss of

tickets and accommodation due to a diving accident, loss of equipment, death as a result of a diving accident, permanent disability and repatriation to your home country. Annual fees start at US$64 (about Dhs.235).

Dive Insurance Contact Details

DAN Europe
www.daneurope.org
+39 85 893 0333
mail@daneurope.org

PADI
www.diveinsurance.com
+ 714 739 3177

Vicencia & Buckley
diverprotection@diveinsurance.org

Activities

Even for non-divers a weekend living on the sea is a wonderful thing. Charter a dhow, throw in your mask and snorkel and start exploring.

Snorkelling

Snorkelling is a great hobby and with the conditions in the UAE consisting of relatively calm waters for most of the year, this is the perfect place to get into it. Whatever your age or fitness levels, snorkelling will get you into the sea and the minute you get your first glimpse of bright reef life, you'll be hooked.

Thanks to their noisy breathing apparatus, divers often tend to scare many marine animals away, or at least keep their distance. Snorkellers though are well-placed to see excellent fish life. Divers often return to the boat to hear of turtles being seen coming up for air on the surface, rays jumping out of the water (apparently to get parasites off their backs) and of shoals of different fish near the surface. In the winter there are some areas where you're almost guaranteed sightings of sharks and, again, snorkellers often strike it luckier than divers.

Benefits

This is a great way for the family to enjoy an activity together, and all you need is some basic equipment and you're ready to go. And unlike divers, when snorkellers see something exciting they can call their buddy over to share the sight.

Equipment

All you need is a pair of fins, a tempered glass mask and a snorkel. There are two types of fins: open foot fins and fins meant to be used with booties. It's also a good idea to wear a suit or a 'skin' (which is thinner than a wetsuit but still offers UV protection) to prevent sunburn and to offer some protection from jellyfish stings. If you wear a wetsuit you may need to wear a weightbelt too, especially if you like to duck dive down and check things out.

You can buy or hire snorkelling equipment from most dive shops or centres (see Dive Directory on p.181) and some hotels. A good dive shop will advise you on how to find a mask that's a good fit, you'll be shown how to attach the snorkel to the mask and assisted in choosing fins that meet your requirements.

Cost

As new pursuits go, snorkelling is not terribly expensive. There's a wide variety of masks and snorkels to be found and they range in price from Dhs.80 for a generic set to Dhs.300 for a branded, diving-specific set.

Getting out to a snorkelling spot can involve some expense, although if you head out from the shore all it costs is a little bit of energy on your part. If you want to go snorkelling on the east coast, there are a number of excellent snorkelling sites and most dive centres will take you out on a dive boat. You can snorkel on the surface, or chill out on a nearby island beach, while the divers head down under. Prices vary but you can expect to pay around Dhs.50-70 for a two-hour trip or so (that's two hours in which you're taken to the site, get to snorkel around it and head back to shore again).

Marine Life

You will see large shoals of reef fish, turtles, rays and even (small) sharks. Don't overlook the corals though: if you take a torch you'll be able to see them in their true colours and the display is often quite amazing.

Snorkelling Sites
West Coast

The only places to snorkel on the west coast are off the harbour walls, but take care: on the outside harbour walls the waves tend to bash against the rocks and

Cement Barge (p.10)
Barracuda Barge (p.8)
Jazirat Sir Bu Na'air (p.26)
Turtle Barge (p.50)

you may get caught off guard by a rogue wave (created by boats in the construction areas). You can snorkel on the inside of the harbour walls, but the water there is rather still and tends to silt up. The fish also prefer the outside walls.

Musandam

Take care when snorkelling in Musandam as there can be unusual currents due to the narrow channel between Oman and Iran (the Strait of Hormuz). It's a good idea to go with a tour company and have a guide to point out the best sites. The best fish life is to be found between the surface and 10m, so try to snorkel along the side of rocks and islands.

There are a number of tour companies that offer dhow trips for dolphin watching and snorkelling. The boats are usually moored in areas that are safe to snorkel in, and you

Try And Buy

Dubai-based snorkellers love Scuba Dubai who allow you to hire equipment on a Thursday and return it on a Saturday, and only charge you for one-day's hire. If you're considering buying a piece of equipment, they'll let you hire it before you buy. If you decide to purchase it, they'll give you the cost of the hire off the price of the item.

dive centre in advance. Depending on your swimming ability and the water conditions,

Dibba Island (p.100)
Hole in the Wall (p.102)
Martini Rock (p.118)
Murbah Reef (p.120)
Ras Qidfa (p.122)
Shark Island (p.126)
Sharm Rocks (p.128)
Snoopy Island (p.130)

you can go to Sandy Beach Motel and spend the day on the beach and swim out to Snoopy Island, just a short distance from shore. In winter time the water recedes a long way and the distance you have to swim is even less.

can even arrange overnight camping trips with these companies. Khasab Tours on the Musandam west coast and Al Marsa on

The Caves (p.62)
Lima Rock (p.66)
Octopus Rock (p.78)
Pearl Island (p.80)
Ras Hamra (p.82)
Ras Lima (p.84)
Ras Marovi (p.86)

the Musandam east coast are some of the operators here (see Dive Directory, p.181).

East Coast

The east coast is a great area for snorkelling and has the most diverse marine life. Most dive centres take snorkellers out on their boats (along with divers and the trip lasts for about two hours in total). Some centres can make arrangements to take you to Shark or Khor Fakkan Island where you can spend the day. They'll come and collect at the time you agree on. If that's what you'd like to do, it's best to arrange this with your

Safety

- If you haven't been snorkelling before, it's a good idea to try your equipment out in a swimming pool before heading into the sea. You need to develop a strong 'huffing' action with your mouth like breathing out very hard in order to push out the water that floods the snorkel when you duck your head underwater.

- It's recommended that you snorkel in pairs for safety reasons.

- Be aware of any boats or jetskis in the area and keep a lookout for these if you're snorkelling off a busy beach.

- Make sure that you're protected against the sun; it's easy to burn your back and legs without even realising it because the water keeps you cool.

- Protect against possible jellyfish stings by wearing a suit.

- Drink plenty of water to prevent becoming dehydrated.

Boat, Yacht and Dhow Charters

Sailing along the coast in a dhow is an atmospheric and memorable way to experience the region's coastal life.

There are a number of companies (see below) that offer dhow, boat or yacht charters. They range from a sundowner cruise of a couple of hours, overnight trips with stopovers for snorkelling to liveaboard type dive excursions.

If you want to do your own thing, large independent groups can charter a dhow from the fishermen at Dibba on the east coast, to travel up the coast to Musandam. If you haggle you can usually knock the price down substantially, especially if you know a bit of Arabic – try saying your proposed price followed by 'mafi mushkila' ('no problem').

Expect to pay around Dhs.2,500 per day for a dhow large enough to take 20 – 25 people, or Dhs.100 per hour for a smaller vessel. You'll need to take your own food and water (and dive gear if you're planning on diving), as nothing is supplied onboard. The dhows are equipped with ice lockers though, which are suitable for storing supplies. Conditions are basic, but you'll have the freedom to plan your own route and to see the beautiful fjord-like scenery of the Musandam from a traditional wooden dhow.

The waters in the area are beautifully clear and turtles and dolphins can often be seen from the boat, although sometimes unfavourable weather conditions can seriously reduce visibility for divers. If you leave from Dibba (or Dabba), Omani visas are not required, even though you enter Omani waters. It's also possible to arrange stops along the coast and it's worth taking camping equipment for the night, although you can sleep on board.

This kind of trip is ideal for diving but you should hire any equipment you may need before you get to Dibba. Non divers in your group can spend the day swimming, snorkelling and soaking up the sun.

Boat, Yacht and Dhow Charter Companies

UAE		
Abu Dhabi		
Arabian Divers	02 665 8742	www.fishabudhabi.com
Dubai		
Charlotte Anne Charters	04 222 9007	www.charlotteannecharters.com
El Mundo	050 452 3202	www.elmundodubai.com
Hormuzline Tours Company	04 266 4541	www.hormuzlinetours.com
Khasab Travel & Tours	04 266 9950	www.khasabtours.com
Yacht Solutions	04 348 6838	www.yacht-solutions.com
Dibba		
Al Marsa Travel & Tourism & Charters	06 544 1232	www.musandamdiving.com
Nomad Ocean Divers	050 885 3238	www.discovernomad.com
Oman		
Khasab		
Hormuzline Tours Company	+968 2673 1616	www.hormuzlinetours.com
Khasab Travel & Tours	+968 2673 0464	www.khasabtours.com
Musandam Sea Adventure Tourism	+968 2673 0069	www.musandam-sea-adventures.com
Muscat		
Arabian Sea Safaris	+968 2469 3223	www.arabianseasafaris.com

First Aid

Hopefully you'll never have any serious (and seriously unpleasant) encounters while out exploring. However, accidents do happen. Here are some basic first aid pointers in case you have a run-in with some marine life.

One excellent reason for not touching anything and keeping your hands to yourself while diving is the number of things down there that can sting or stab you – many of which are also cunningly camouflaged. Most marine creatures are not aggressive and would rather flee than attack, but if you unwittingly threaten them by standing on them, touching them or venturing into their territory (or even, sometimes, by trying to take a photograph of them!) the result can be a painful and potentially serious injury.

What follows is a brief guide to dealing with hazardous marine life. For a full picture, it's best to refer to a comprehensive first aid book – you'll find a list of books in the Bibliography on p.179. Bites and stings can be serious, and the tricky part is that you often don't know exactly what you've been bitten or stung by. When you're unsure, seek medical assistance immediately. Turn to p.151 for a list of emergency contact numbers.

All The Small Things

Many tiny things, that you probably haven't even noticed touching, can cause irritation, itchiness or a rash. For example, an attractive coral that looks like a fern or fan is a hydrocoral and it can actually deliver a nasty burn, especially if you happen to be susceptible to it.

If you're the kind of person who suffers an allergic reaction to bee stings, ant bites or jellyfish, it's wise to steer clear of everything in the water, keep a first aid kit on land and always wear protection in the water in the form of a wetsuit, even in the summer months. If you don't manage to avoid contact with things that sting and you develop a mild reaction, you can try antihistamine or steroid creams to treat the itch or irritation.

Catfish

Catfish have three spines attached to their dorsal and lateral fins. They're not aggressive and won't attack but they are dangerous to touch.

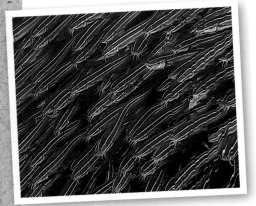

- Control bleeding
- Immobilise limb
- Medical attention or hospitalisation may be required

Cone Shell

During the day, most cone shells bury themselves in the sand, emerging at

night to search for food. Their weapon is a harpoon-like poison dart that they 'fire' when they spot a potential meal and inject into the victim. Each shell has a number of harpoons, which are made of a hard, bone-like substance and measure about a centimetre in length. You're most likely to

be stung by a cone shell if you pick it up. Cone shells occur on the west, east and Musandam coasts.

Of the hundreds of species of cone shells, only a few are believed to be dangerous. The effect can range from painless, to excruciating and the venom causes muscle paralysis. Salt water seems to make the pain worse.

- Apply pressure bandages, painkillers and CPR
- Wash the wound with hot water (45-50°C) – the wound will have a milky appearance
- Immobilise the limb
- Heart failure can occur in severe cases – so seek medical attention immediately

Crown of Thorns Starfish

These starfish measure up to 60cm in diameter and have 13 to 16 arms covered in sharp spines that can inflict a nasty, and painful wound. They prey on corals and are usually found in water deeper than other starfish seem to like. The spines can cause bleeding, inflammation and secondary infection. If the spines aren't removed the symptoms can continue for weeks or months.

- Wash wound with hot water
- Immobilise or make the victim lie down

- Remove the spines
- In serious cases the broken-off spines may have to be surgically removed

Flower Urchin
(Toxopneustes)
While the black spiny urchin is the most common type of urchin and more likely to

cause injury thanks to its longer spines, its cousin the flower urchin is far more dangerous. It looks like it's covered in flowers, but these are actually tiny pincers that pack a venomous punch.
- Wash wound with hot water (45-50°C)
- Immobilise limb or lay victim down
- Remove spines
- Seek medical attention immediately

Hydroid Coral
Hyrdoid corals look like feathery plants, but they're actually colonies of animals that contain nematocysts (stinging cells) that they use to capture their next meal, and for defence. Divers are particularly

prone to brushing against these corals and you'll want to avoid the fine white feathery ones and the dense yellow-brown types in particular. The sting is irritating and painful, but generally not serious.
- Apply vinegar or alcohol spirit

Jellyfish
There are thousands of marine species that use nematocysts (stinging capsules) as a

defense – including corals, anemones and jellyfish. Contact with a jellyfish can result in anything from a mild, localised itch, to severe burning and throbbing pain or even cardio-respiratory difficulties. It's difficult to know which jellyfish is dangerous and which isn't, but one school of thought is that coloured jellyfish (that appear in September and October in particular) have a bad sting. The extremely dangerous boxfish or deadly sea wasp doesn't occur in Gulf waters.

- Do not rub wound
- Remove tentacles
- Wash surface of the wound
- Apply ice pack, then vinegar, ammonia or alcohol spirit
- In rare cases, severe stings have arrested breathing and caused heart failure – seek medical attention

Lionfish

These beautiful fish are not aggressive, although they can be territorial at times. Their long spines contain venom that causes intense pain.

Moray Eel

These rather scary looking creatures can grow to 6 to 8 feet in length, and their razor sharp teeth mean a bite will bleed profusely and often becomes infected. But for all their appearances, morays aren't aggressive. They can become territorial though, and will object to being teased.

- Apply pressure bandages and painkillers
- Control the bleeding
- Immobilise the limb
- As serious secondary infection can occur, hospitalisation is required

You're most likely to be accidentally hurt by putting your hand into crevices or not watching where you place your hands while exploring a reef – lionfish particularly enjoy the shelter of an overhang, which makes them difficult to spot.

- Wash wound with hot water (45-50°C)
- Control bleeding
- Administer painkillers
- Venom causes intense pain and breathing difficulties – seek medical attention immediately

Dive Medical Kit

Cuts & Wounds
Adhesive dressing and tape, plasters, antiseptic cream

Dehydration
Salt sachet (e.g. Dioralyte), isotonic drinks, water

Marine Stings
Vinegar, sodium bicarbonate, powdered meat tenderiser or any powder

Seasickness
Sturgeron, Dezinil or Dramamine

General
Tweezers, scissors, sterile or saline water, personal medication

Nematocyst

Nematocysts are stinging cells or capsules used by marine creatures like coral, jellyfish and anemones. Some nudibranch species

feed on nematocysts and incorporate the effects into their own defence system. The symptoms range from mild skin irritation to intense pain. If a large patch of the skin is exposed, the victim could suffer from nausea and vomiting.

- Gently remove any nematocysts that may still be stuck to the skin (don't squeeze them as this will discharge more nematocysts)
- Apply local anaesthetic spray or ointment
- If breathing becomes impaired seek medical attention
- Give CPR if needed
- Victims might experience intense itching a few days after the event – a steroid cream might help

Octopus

Octopus don't usually attack people but there have been a few recorded incidents where divers have been bitten. Octopus have a beak that they will use to hunt and to defend themselves with, and they can inject a mild venom. They're most likely to bite if stepped on or picked up.

- Milk wound
- Apply pressure bandages
- Immobilise limb and keep it lower than the head and heart
- Administer CPR if necessary and seek medical attention immediately

Avoidance tactics

- Avoid close encounters
- Watch where you put your hands and be aware of your surroundings.
- Practice buoyancy control.
- Wear protective gear.
- Aim to be a passive observer and don't touch or tease marine life.
- Know your limits – when you're out of your depth (literally, in the case of divers), you're more likely to make clumsy mistakes.
- Avoid holding onto a buoy line without gloves as jellyfish and other stinging creatures can get caught on the line.

Stingray

Stingrays aren't aggressive but can cause excruciating pain if accidentally stepped on, or handled (when fishermen remove them from their nets, for instance). They

- Apply CPR, pressure bandages
- Administer painkillers
- Make victim lie down or immobilise them
- The sting can cause fatal paralysis and cardiac arrest – you should seek medical attention immediately

lie on or near the bottom of the sea and often submerge themselves in the sand. If given half the chance, a ray will swim off, so to avoid stepping on one when you go swimming, shuffle your feet in shallow water, warning them of your approach. The sting can cause deep lacerations and profuse bleeding.

- Apply pressure bandage to stop bleeding (this may take a while)
- Immerse limb in hot water
- Seek medical attention immediately
- Make sure the patient has a tetanus shot if their last one was more than five years previously
- Secondary infection can occur after 24 hours – if the wound becomes more red and painful see a doctor

Scorpionfish

Like stonefish, many scorpionfish look like rocks and they also have venomous spines. They're most likely to cause injury if stepped on or picked up. Although not as dangerous as stonefish, they should be treated the same way.

- Milk wound
- Immobilise limb

Sea Snake

Sea snakes are shy and not likely to attack. They also have very small mouths and aren't able to bite large prey. That said, their poison is 20 times more powerful than that of a cobra, but they inject less of it, if any at all, when they bite. Sea snakes live in all tropical waters, except the Atlantic and they're distinguished from land snakes and eels by the flat tail that they use for swimming.

- Milk wound
- Apply pressure bandages, CPR
- Immobilise victim or lay them down
- Keep limb lower than head and heart
- The venomous bite can cause fatal paralysis and cardiac arrest – seek medical attention immediately

Sea Urchin

The spines of the sea urchin contain venom so watch where you place your hands or feet, especially on rocky snorkelling or

diving sites, or if you're exploring a tidal pool. In the UAE you're most likely to encounter urchins on the east coast. The spines can cause mild to severe pain that lasts for a few hours, and the chances of a secondary infection are high. However, very few fatalities have been reported and these have generally been as a result of respiratory problems.

- Do not rub wound or remove spines as they might break off in the skin
- Wash wound with water as hot as the victim can take it (40-50°C)
- Apply vinegar or alcohol spirit
- In most cases the body will break the spines down and dissolve them, but in rare instances they may need to be removed surgically

Stonefish

A fish with a tough, warty skin, the stonefish is usually the colour of its surroundings so it's difficult to spot,

but it's only dangerous if stepped on or caught. The stonefish has 13 dorsal spines and when trodden on, these penetrate the skin, injecting venom into the foot. The pain is excruciating and can last for months. Stonefish tend to occur mostly on the UAE's east coast.

- Remove pieces of spines
- Milk the wound – encouraging bleeding might remove some of the venom
- Wash with hot water and immerse wound for 30-90 minutes if possible.
- Immobilise and elevate the limb
- Apply pressure bandages
- Administer painkillers and immobilise the victim or make them lie down
- The venom can cause fatal paralysis and cardiac arrest - you need to seek medical attention immediately

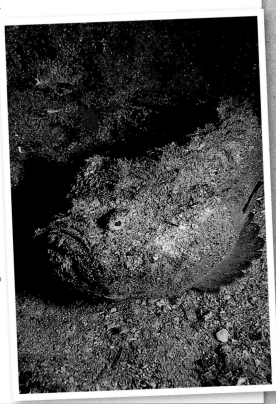

GPS Coordinates

The GPS is now the preferred navigation system for divers to find their dive sites. We have given coordinates for all the dive sites covered and many of the popular harbours and launch sites.

Although we now all depend on the GPS receiver, we have also supplied distances and headings to and from dive sites and harbours to assist in dead reckoning navigation in the unlikely event of GPS failure.

Coordinates

The coordinates for each dive site here are given in degrees, minutes and seconds (dd°mm' ss.s").

Map datum

We have used WGS84 (World Geodetic System 84) datum. The map datum affects the relative accuracy between coordinates

obtained in one map datum and used in a GPS using a different map datum. All maps have a map datum and there are more than one hundred different data used to accommodate local regional irregularities.

Given the difference it makes, it's important that your GPS receiver is set to the same datum as the coordinates you are entering into it. The difference between one map datum being entered into a GPS received using another map datum, can be as much as 200m.

Most GPS receivers default datum is WGS84. In the setup of your GPS receiver, you can select regional map data. The Admiralty charts worldwide use WGS84, but it's also useful to know that the UAE regional datum is Nahrwn United Arab Emirates and the Ordnance Survey Great Britain is OSGB.

Dive site coordinates

	Dive	Name	GPS	Page
	1	Anchor Barge	N25°30'47.6" E55°04'35.7"	6
	2	Barracuda Barge	N25°27'15.6" E55°22'41.4"	8
	3	Cement Barge	N25°10'19.7" E55°12'17.7"	10
	4	Energy Determination	N26°04'08.1" E55°34'04.1"	14
	5	Hammour Barge	N25°04'40.5" E54°46'06.5"	18
W E S T C O A S T	6	Hopper Barge	N25°30'27.9" E55°03'58.6"	20
	7	Jasim	N24°58'47.2" E54°29'43.8"	24
	8	Jazirat Sir Bu Na'air	N25°13'30.0" E54°13'00.0"	26
	9	Lion City	N25°00'13.4" E54°31'43.9"	28
	10	Mariam Express	N25°27'19.7" E55°06'16.0"	30
	11	MV Dara	N25°34'29.0" E55°27'58.6"	36
	12	MV Hannan	N24°50'11.0" E53°53'34.0"	38
	13	MV Ludwig	N25°06'53.8" E54°34'14.1"	40
	14	Nasteran	N25°28'00.0" E55°21'22.0"	42
	15	Neptune	N25°30'22.0" E55°03'55.0 "	44
	16	Swift	N25°27'37.7" E54°17'41.2"	48
	17	Turtle Barge	N25°26'43.2" E55°26'57.6"	50
	18	Zainab	N25°14'55.8" E54°51'32.4"	52
	19	The Caves	N25°48'14.4" E56°22'03.0"	62
	20	Landing Craft	N26°12'40.0" E56°17'05.1"	64
	21	Lima Rock	N25°56'27.2" E56°27'51.2"	66
M U S A N D A M	22	Bu Rashid	N26°24'12.0" E56°29'42.0"	69
	23	Ennerdale Rock	N26°27'39.5" E56°30'57.2"	69
	24	Fanaku Island	N26°29'55.1" E56°31'50.4"	70
	25	Great Quion Island	N26°30'21.0" E56°30'51.6"	70
	26	Hard Rock Café	N26°12'13.0" E56°29'18.5"	71
	27	Jazirat Al Khayl	N26°22'24.0" E56°26'51.0"	71
	28	Jazirat Hamra	N26°16'54.0" E56°27'12.0"	71
	29	Jazirat Sawda	N26°17'43.6" E56°27'12.5"	71
	30	Jazirat Musandam East Head	N26°22'11.0" E56°32'18.0"	72
	31	Jazirat Umm Al Fayyarin	N26°10'31.9" E56°32'47.2"	72
	32	Kachalu Island	N26°23'45.5" E56°31'48.1"	73

	Dive	Name	GPS	Page
M U S A N D A M	33	Ras Dillah	N26°07'51.0" E56°29'16.2"	73
	34	Ras Dillah Ghubbat Ash Shabus Bay	N26°08'37.3" E56°28'47.1"	74
	35	Ras Khaysay	N26°14'00.0" E56°29'24.0"	74
	36	Ras Musandam	N26°23'12.1" E56°31'29.1"	74
	37	Ras Qabr Al Hindi	N26°18'33.8" E56°30'52.1"	75
	38	Ras Sarkan	N26°05'17.3" E56°28'18.7"	75
	39	Ruqq Suwayk	N26°24'11.9" E56°28'42.1"	76
	40	White Rock	N26°14'11.9" E56°29'42.6"	76
	41	Octopus Rock	N26°00'01.2" E56°26'20.4"	78
	42	Pearl Island	N25°57'36.6" E56°25'51.9"	80
	43	Ras Hamra	N25°55'20.7" E56°26'38.7"	82
	44	Ras Lima	N25°56'46.2" E56°27'30.7"	84
	45	Ras Marovi	N25°59'06.0" E56°26'09.0"	86
E A S T C O A S T	46	Anemone Gardens	N25°21'01.3" E56°22'46.9"	92
	47	Car Cemetery	N25°25'07.0" E56°22'34.2"	94
	48	Coral Gardens	N25°21'12.0" E56°22'48.0"	96
	49	Deep Reef	N25°04'02.7" E56°24'25.6"	98
	50	Dibba Island	N25°36'14.1" E56°21'05.9"	100
	51	Hole in the Wall	N25°20'26.3" E56°22'39.7"	102
	52	Inchcape 1	N25°30'44.8" E56°22'56.7"	104
	53	Inchcape 2	N25°20'19.8" E56°22'53.3"	108
	54	Inchcape 10	N25°07'36.1" E56°23'05.3"	114
	55	Ines	N25°11'21.8" E56°27'30.6"	116
	56	Martini Rock	N25°20'05.2" E56°22'53.0 "	118
	57	Murbah Reef	N25°16'21.0" E56°22'31.6"	120
	58	Ras Qidfa	N25°19'27.2" E56°22'56.0"	122
	59	Refinery Reef	N25°18'22.7" E56°23'10.9"	124
	60	Shark Island	N25°21'12.0" E56°22'36.2"	126
	61	Sharm Rocks	N25°28'55.0" E56°21'57.1"	128
	62	Snoopy Island	N25°29'29.0" E56°21'59.0"	130

Note:
The map data used in the Underwater Explorer for all dive sites coordinates is WGS84, the World Geodetic System 84. Please ensure you select this option in your GPS receiver set-up.

Harbour Locations

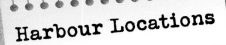

West Coast
The Club Slipway, Abu Dhabi
GPS: N24°30'46" E54°23'18"

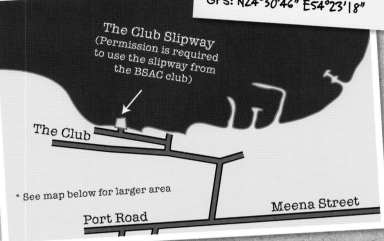

The Club Slipway
(Permission is required
to use the slipway from
the BSAC club)

The Club

* See map below for larger area

Port Road

Meena Street

West Coast
Public Slipway, Abu Dhabi
GPS: N29°30'45" E54°22'26"

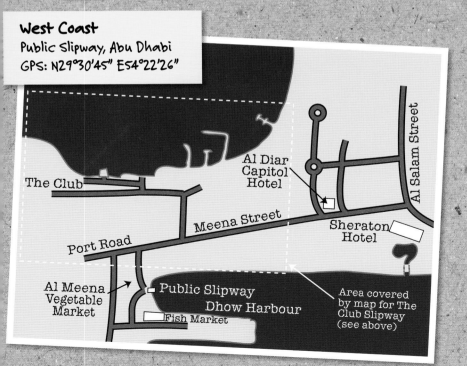

The Club

Al Diar
Capitol
Hotel

Al Salam Street

Meena Street

Sheraton
Hotel

Port Road

Al Meena
Vegetable
Market

Public Slipway
Dhow Harbour

Fish Market

Area covered
by map for The
Club Slipway
(see above)

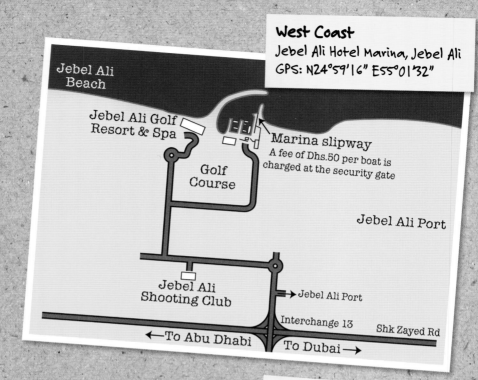

West Coast
Jebel Ali Hotel Marina, Jebel Ali
GPS: N24°59'16" E55°01'32"

Jebel Ali Beach

Jebel Ali Golf Resort & Spa

Marina slipway
A fee of Dhs.50 per boat is charged at the security gate

Golf Course

Jebel Ali Port

Jebel Ali Shooting Club

Jebel Ali Port

Interchange 13

Shk Zayed Rd

← To Abu Dhabi

To Dubai →

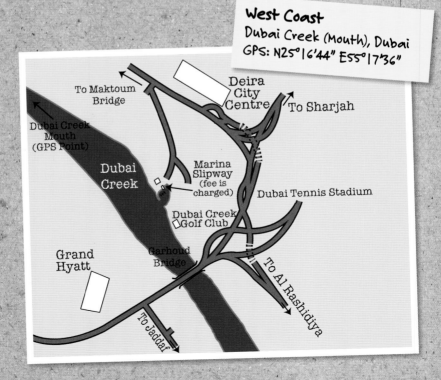

West Coast
Dubai Creek (Mouth), Dubai
GPS: N25°16'44" E55°17'36"

To Maktoum Bridge

Deira City Centre

To Sharjah

Dubai Creek Mouth (GPS Point)

Dubai Creek

Marina Slipway (fee is charged)

Dubai Tennis Stadium

Dubai Creek Golf Club

Grand Hyatt

Garhoud Bridge

To Al Rashidiya

To Jaddaf

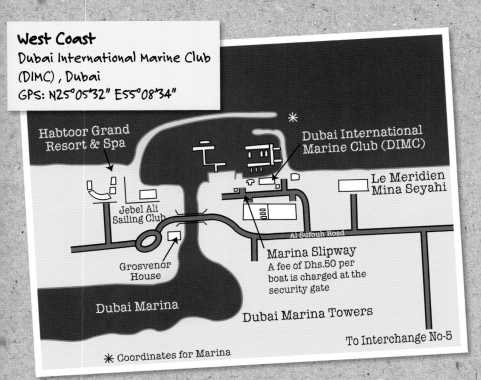

West Coast
Dubai International Marine Club
(DIMC) , Dubai
GPS: N25°05'32" E55°08'34"

Habtoor Grand
Resort & Spa

Dubai International
Marine Club (DIMC)

Le Meridien
Mina Seyahi

Jebel Ali
Sailing Club

Al Sufouh Road

Grosvenor
House

Marina Slipway
A fee of Dhs.50 per
boat is charged at the
security gate

Dubai Marina

Dubai Marina Towers

To Interchange No-5

✳ Coordinates for Marina

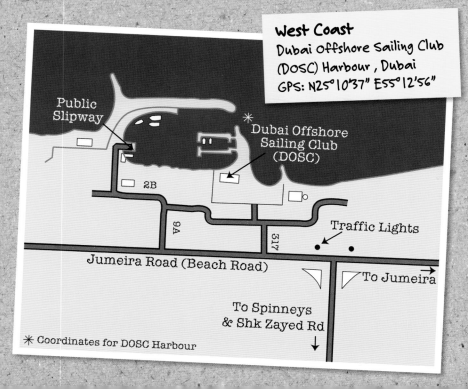

West Coast
Dubai Offshore Sailing Club
(DOSC) Harbour , Dubai
GPS: N25°10'37" E55°12'56"

Public
Slipway

Dubai Offshore
Sailing Club
(DOSC)

2B

9A

317

Traffic Lights

Jumeira Road (Beach Road)

To Jumeira

To Spinneys
& Shk Zayed Rd

✳ Coordinates for DOSC Harbour

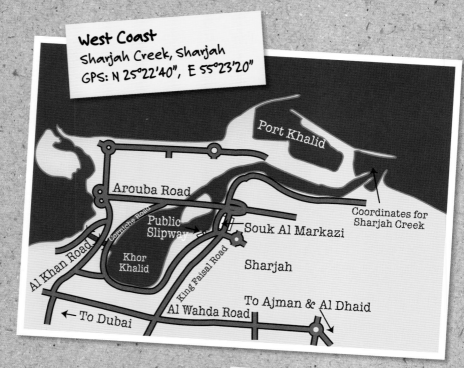

West Coast
Sharjah Creek, Sharjah
GPS: N 25°22'40", E 55°23'20"

Port Khalid

Arouba Road

Coordinates for
Sharjah Creek

Corniche Road

Public
Slipway

Souk Al Markazi

Al Khan Road

Khor
Khalid

King Faisal Road

Sharjah

To Ajman & Al Dhaid

← To Dubai

Al Wahda Road

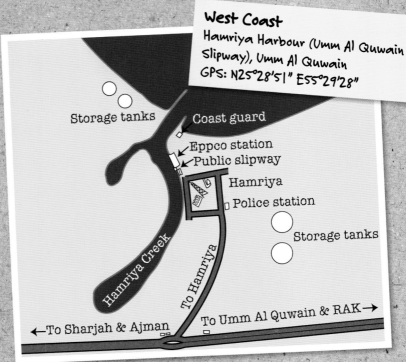

West Coast

Hamriya Harbour (Umm Al Quwain
Slipway), Umm Al Quwain
GPS: N25°28'51" E55°29'28"

Storage tanks

Coast guard

Eppco station
Public slipway

Hamriya

Police station

Storage tanks

Hamriya Creek

To Hamriya

←To Sharjah & Ajman

To Umm Al Quwain & RAK →

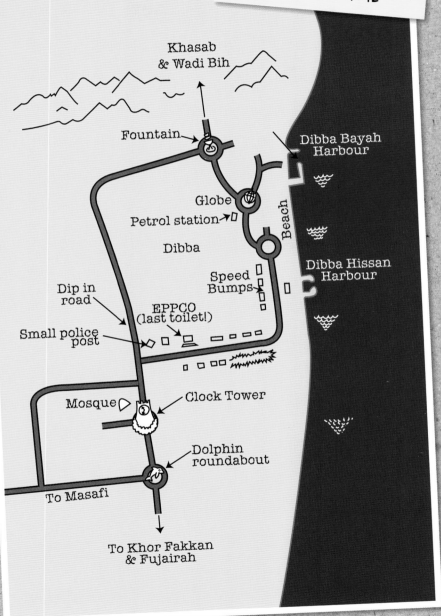

East Coast
Dibba Bayah Harbour, Dibba
(For Musandam)
GPS: N25°39'04" E56°16'12"

Khasab
& Wadi Bih

Fountain

Dibba Bayah
Harbour

Globe

Petrol station

Dibba

Beach

Dibba Hissan
Harbour

Speed
Bumps

Dip in
road

EPPCO
(last toilet!)

Small police
post

Mosque

Clock Tower

Dolphin
roundabout

To Masafi

To Khor Fakkan
& Fujairah

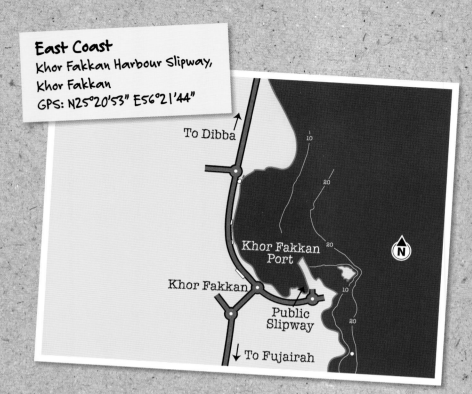

East Coast
Khor Fakkan Harbour Slipway,
Khor Fakkan
GPS: N25°20'53" E56°21'44"

To Dibba

10

20

Khor Fakkan
Port

20

Khor Fakkan

10

Public
Slipway

20

To Fujairah

N

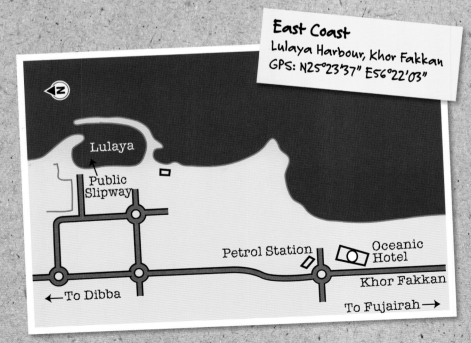

East Coast
Lulaya Harbour, Khor Fakkan
GPS: N25°23'37" E56°22'03"

N

Lulaya

Public
Slipway

Petrol Station

Oceanic
Hotel

Khor Fakkan

← To Dibba

To Fujairah →

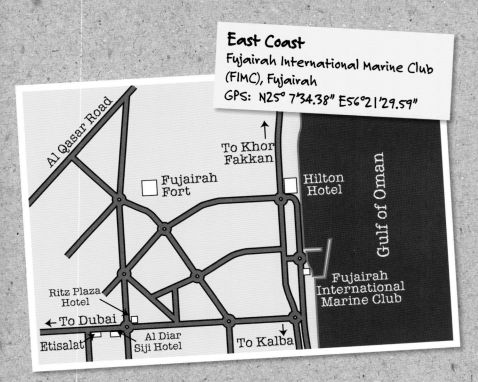

East Coast
Fujairah International Marine Club
(FIMC), Fujairah
GPS: N25° 7'34.38" E56°21'29.59"

Al Qasar Road

To Khor
Fakkan

Fujairah
Fort

Hilton
Hotel

Gulf of Oman

Fujairah
International
Marine Club

Ritz Plaza
Hotel

← To Dubai

Etisalat

Al Diar
Siji Hotel

To Kalba

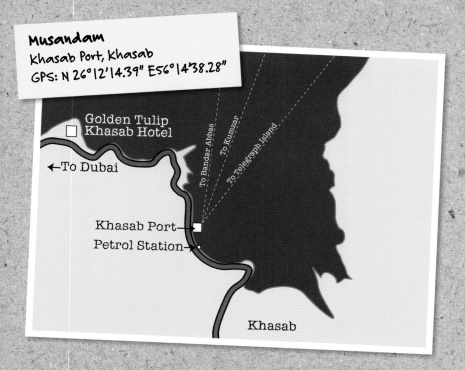

Musandam
Khasab Port, Khasab
GPS: N 26°12'14.39" E56°14'38.28"

Golden Tulip
Khasab Hotel

← To Dubai

To Bandar Abbas

To Kumzar

To Telegraph Island

Khasab Port—

Petrol Station—

Khasab

Harbour Locations

Shipping Weights and Measures

Displacement Tonnage

This is the weight of the water displaced by the boat. It's equal to the weight of the boat and all that is in her; therefore it varies with her draft. Displacement in tonnes = volume of water displaced (in cubic feet), divided by 35 or 36 (depending on whether the water is salt or fresh). Displacement may also be quoted in tonnage.

35 cubic feet of salt water weighs 1 tonne
36 cubic feet of fresh water weighs 1 tonne
1 cubic foot = 0.0283 cubic metres
1 cubic metre = 35.31 cubic feet
1 tonne = 2,240 pounds or 1,000 kilograms

Dead-weight (DWT)

This is the weight of the cargo, stores, fuel, passengers and crew when the boat is loaded to her maximum summer load line. It's expressed in pounds, tonnes or kilograms.

Gross Tonnage

The gross tonnage is measured according to the law of the national authority with which the vessel is registered. Broadly speaking, the measurement is the capacity of all the spaces within the hull, and enclosed spaces above the deck available for cargo, stores, passengers and crew (with certain exceptions), divided by 100. The amount is expressed in cubic feet.

Net Tonnage

This figure is derived by deducting the space used for the accommodation of the crew, navigation equipment, machinery and fuel from the figure for the vessel's gross tonnage.

Builder's Measure

Until 1873, the tonnage of a vessel was called Builders Measurement (BM). This was more than likely based on the number of casks the vessel could carry. After 1873, displacement tonnage was used. From about 1926 onwards, the actual weight has been calibrated. Data on some vessels is shown in BM, but over time this number has been converted to actual tonnes and may not be precise – in other words, a vessel shown as 100BM is not automatically 100 tonnes.

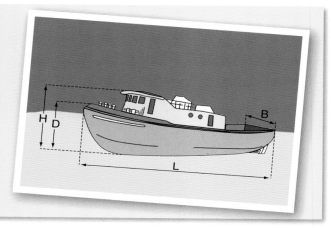

Dimensions	
Length (L) – length from stern to bow	
Breadth (B) – length of beam from port to starboard	
Depth (D) – depth from deck to keel	
Height (H) – height from keel to the top of the bridge	

Wreck Data

Wherever possible we have supplied information about each wreck. Data has been obtained either from the Lloyds Register of Shipping or from the Hydrographic List.

Wreck Register	The number allocated to the wreck by Lloyds or the Hydrographic Society
Name	The original name of the vessel
Nationality	The name of the country or flag that the boat sailed under
Year built	The year the vessel was built
Type	The boat may have been one of the following types: cargo vessel, coastal barge, coastal tanker, coastal vessel, landing craft, motor lighter, passenger liner, tug, very large crude container
Tonnage	Refer to information on Shipping Weights and Measures (opposite)
Cargo	What the boat was carrying at the time of loss
Date sunk	When the vessel was sunk
Depth	Depth where the wreckage lies

Lloyd's List

Up until 1741, there was no centralised source of information on shipwrecks. Details were kept locally, and information on a limited number of incidents was traceable through secondary sources, such as a checklist of narratives of shipwrecks and disasters at sea.

A daily record on information on shipping casualties is available from 1741, the year of the oldest surviving issue of the Lloyd's List. As the Lloyd's of London's intelligence network grew, so the List became increasingly comprehensive, covering not only British vessels and wrecks in British waters, but shipping losses worldwide.

From 1856 onwards, reports of inquiries were also published in newspapers, most notably Mitchell's Maritime Register, 1856-1884, and the Shipping Gazette (Lloyd's List Weekly Summary).

A variety of indexes is available from the Guildhall Library in London. These and other records of losses are described in the second edition of the Guide to the Lloyd's Marine Collection by Declan Barriskill.

'Posted' editions of the Lloyd's Register of Ships often indicated the fate of a vessel – 'collision', 'foundered', 'condemned' or so on. Sometimes the year and the month are added (3.89) and refer to the relevant quarter of the Lloyd's Register Casualty Return, published from 1890 to date. The Casualty Returns are available for research at Lloyd's Register in London.

The Mercantile Navy List is never posted but, from 1875 to 1904 lists of vessels removed from the British register are included, with brief reasons why. Separate monthly returns that listed vessels added or removed were also printed. The Public Records Office in Surrey, UK, has bound volumes of these for the period 1875 to 1890 while the Guildhall Library has them for 1890 to 1946. These are particularly useful for vessels not actually lost at sea, but hulked, laid up or condemned.

Glossary

Aft	The area towards the stern of the boat
Beam	The greatest width of the boat
Bow	The area towards the front of the boat
Bridge	The location from which a vessel is steered and its speed controlled
Bulkhead	A vertical partition separating compartments
Buoy	An anchored float used for marking a mooring or position in the water
Deck	A permanent covering over a compartment, hull or any part thereof
Draft	The depth of water a boat draws
DWT	Dead-weight
GPS	Global positioning system (satellite navigation system)
Hatch	An opening in a boat's deck, fitted with a watertight cover
Hold	A compartment below deck in a large vessel, used solely for cargo
Hull	The main body of a vessel
LC	Landing craft
MV	Motor vessel
Nautical mile	One minute of latitude; approximately 6,076 feet (1,852m) – about 1/8 longer than a statute mile of 5,280 feet
Neap tides	The least tidal movement. This occurs twice a month when the moon is at a right angle to the sun; this happens on the moon's first and third quarters. When the combined gravitational pull of both the moon and the sun is the weakest this creates the lowest high water and the highest low water tides.
Port	The left side of a boat with bow in front (red light)
Reciprocal	After travelling from A to B, the opposite bearing to return from B to A
Screw	The boat's propeller
Spring Tides	The greatest tidal movement. This occurs twice a month when the moon and the sun are in line; this happens on new and full moons. When the combined gravitational pull of both the moon and the sun is the strongest this creates the highest high water and the lowest low water tides.
Starboard	The right side of a boat with bow in front (green light)
Stern	The back area of the boat
Thermoclines	A layer of colder water sandwiched between the warmer well-mixed surface water layer and the colder denser lower layer. Seasonal thermoclines form layers in the shallower depths
VLCC	Very large crude carrier

Bibliography

Shipwrecks

- *Dictionary of Disasters at Sea during the Age of Steam*, by Charles Hocking (Lloyd's Register of Shipping, 1969)

- Hydrographic Department, Ministry of Defence, Taunton, Somerset TA12 2DN, United Kingdom. They provide an information service for commercial, private, Ministry of Defence and other government department enquiries. The wreck section has information on all post-1913 marine casualties occurring in continental shelf areas, except for American and Australian coastal waters. A search fee is charged.

- Information Group, Lloyd's Register of Shipping, 100 Leadenhall Street, London EC3A 3BP, United Kingdom. Brief ship details, date and place of losses recorded in quarterly returns, post 1890. This small specialist library also includes some books on shipwrecks. Open to the public.

- *Last Hours of the* Dara by PJ Abraham (Peter Davies, 1963)

- Lloyd's Marine Collection, Guildhall Library, Aldermanbury, London EC2P 2EJ, United Kingdom. Information on marine casualties and shipping movements worldwide from about 1740. Sources include Lloyd's List and war loss records. Open to the public.

- *Modern Shipping Disasters 1963 – 1987* by Norman Hooke (Lloyd's of London Press, 1989)

- *The Grey Widow-Maker* by Bernard Edward (R Hale, 1990)

Marine Life

- *Asia Pacific Reef Guide* by Helmut Debelius (IKAN, available at Scuba Dubai)

- *Coral Reef Animals of the Indo-Pacific* by Terrence M Gosliner, David W Behrens & Gary C Williams (order from Sea Challengers, www.seachallengers.com)

- *Coral Sea Reef Guide* by Bob Halstead (available at Scuba Dubai)

- *Coral Seas of Muscat* (order from Sea Challengers, www.seachallengers.com)

- *Indian Ocean Reef Guide* by Helmut Debelius (IKAN, available at Scuba Dubai)

- *Indo-Pacific Coral Reef Field Guide* by Dr Gerald R Allen & Roger Steene (ISBN 981-00-5687-7, order from Sea Challengers, www.seachallengers.com)

- *Nudibranchs & Sea Snails* by Helmut Debelius (IKAN, available at Scuba Dubai)

- *Red Sea Reef Guide* by Helmut Debelius (Circle Books, available at Scuba Dubai)

- *Reef Fishes UAE and Gulf of Oman* by Richard F Field (Motivate Publishing)

- *Seashells of Oman* by Donald & Eloise Bosch (ISBN 0-582-78309-7, order online from Sea Challengers, www.seachallengers.com)

- *The Coral Seas of Muscat* by Frances Green & Richard Keech (ISBN 0-946510-28-8, order from Sea Challengers, www.seachallengers.com)

First Aid & Safety

- *A Medical Guide to Hazardous Marine Life* by Paul S Auerbach (Best Publishing, ISBN 0-941-33255-1)

- *Red Sea Safety – Guide To Dangerous Marine Animals* by Dr Peter Vine (Immel Publishing) (ISBN 0-907-15112-4)

- *The Diving Emergency Handbook* by John Lippmann & Stan Bugg (ISBN 0-946-02018-3)

Dive Directory

West Coast

Abu Dhabi
Abu Dhabi Sub Aqua Club	02 673 1111	www.the-club.com
◆ Al Masaood ▶ p.IFC, p.5, p.59, p.180, p.IBC	02 642 4222	www.masaoodmarine.com
◆ Arabian Divers ▶ p.vi	050 614 6931	www.diveabudhabi.com
◆ Blue Dolphin Company	02 666 9392	www.interconti.com
◆ Gulf Marine Sports	02 671 0017	www.gulfmarinesports.com
Nautica Environmental Associates	02 676 2086	nautica@eim.ae

Ajman
◆ Blue Planet Diving	06 745 1555	www.ajmankempinski.com

Al Ain
◆ Diversity Scuba	050 335 7567	info@diversityscuba.net

Dubai
◆ Al Boom Diving	04 342 2993	www.alboomdiving.com
◆ Al Masaood ▶ p.IFC, p.5, p.59, p.180, p.IBC	04 324 1544	www.masaoodmarine.com
British Sub Aqua Club	050 536 3649	www.desertsportsdivingclub.com
Charlotte Anne Charters	04 222 9007	tours@segrex.ae
Emirates Diving Ass. ▶ p.iv	04 393 9390	www.emiratesdiving.com
◆ Gulf Marine Sports	04 303 9773	www.gulfmarinesports.com
Neptune Diving ▶ p.xii	04 288 1163	www.supersportsdubai.com
◆ The Pavilion Dive Centre ▶ p.vii	04 406 8827	www.thepaviliondivecentre.com
◆ Scuba Dubai ▶ p.ix	04 331 7433	www.scubadubai.com
◆ Scubatec	04 3348988	www.scubatec.net
Technical Diving Int. Center	04 393 0303	www.tdicenter.com

Ras Al Khaimah
◆ Beach Club Dive Center	07 233 7558	clubdive@eim.ae

Sharjah
Sharjah Wanderers Dive Club	06 566 2105	www.sharjahwanderers.com

East Coast

Al Aqqa
Sandy Beach Diving Centre ▶ p.132	09 244 5050	www.sandybm.com

Dibba
Al Madhani Sea Tourist & Diving	09 690 5080	madhani@hotmail.com
◆ Al Marsa Travel & Tourism ▶ p.54	06 544 1232	www.musandamdiving.com

◆ Freestyle Divers   09 244 5756   www.freestyledivers.com
  Maku Dive Center   09 244 5747   www.geocities.com/maku_divecenter
  Nomad Ocean Adventures   050 885 3238   www.discovernomad.com
  Scuba 2000 ▶ p.88   09 238 8477   www.scuba-2000.com

Fujairah
◆ Scuba International   09 222 0060   www.scubainternational.net

Khor Fakkan
  7 Seas Divers   09 238 7400   www.7seasdivers.com
◆ Divers Down ▶ p.v   09 237 0299   www.diversdown.ae
◆ Diving House ▶ p.xxiv   09 238 3638   dive4fun@eim.ae

Musandam

  Extra Divers   +968 2673 0501   www.extra-divers.li
  Hormuzline Tours Company   +968 2673 1616   www.hormuzlinetours.com
  Khasab Travel & Tours   +968 2673 0464   www.khasabtours.com

Hotel and Resort Directory

West Coast   ● Has dive centre

Abu Dhabi
★★★★★
  Al Diar Capital Hotel   02 678 7700   www.aldiarhotel.com
● Beach Rotana Hotel & Towers   02 644 3000   www.rotana.com
  Hilton Baynunah Tower   02 632 7777   www.hilton.com
  Hilton International Abu Dhabi   02 681 1900   www.hilton.com
  Hotel InterContinental Abu Dhabi   02 666 6888   www.intercontinental.com
  Le Royal Meridien Hotel   02 674 2020   www.lemeridien.com
  Millennium Hotel   02 626 2700   www.milleniumhotels.com
  Sheraton Abu Dhabi
  Resort & Towers   02 677 3333   www.sheraton.com/abudhabi

★★★★
  Al Ain Palace Hotel   02 679 4777   www.alainpalacehotel.com
  Al Diar Dana Hotel   02 645 6000   www.aldiarhotels.com
  Dhafra Beach Hotel   02 877 1600   www.ncth.com
● Golden Tulip Al Jazira Hotel & Resort 02 562 9100 www.goldentulipaljazira.com

Ajman
★★★★
● Ajman Kempinski Hotel & Resort   06 745 1555   www.ajman.kempinski.com

Dubai

★★★★★

- Al Qasr   04 366 8888   www.jumeirah.com
  Burj Al Arab   04 301 7777   www.burj-al-arab.com
  Dubai Marine Beach Resort & Spa   04 346 1111   www.dxbmarine.com
  Habtoor Grand Resort & Spa   04 399 5000   www.habtoorhotels.com
  Hilton Dubai Jumeirah   04 399 1111   www.hilton.com
  Hyatt Regency Hotel   04 209 1234   www.dubai.regency.hyatt.com
  Jebel Ali Golf Resort & Spa   04 883 6000   www.jebelalihotel.com
  Jumeirah Beach Club
  Resort & Spa   04 344 5333   www.jumeirah.com
- Jumeirah Beach Hotel   04 348 0000   www.jumeirah.com
  Le Meridien Mina Seyahi
  Beach Resort & Marina   04 399 3333   www.lemeridien-minaseyahi.com
  Mina A'Salam   04 3668888   www.jumeirah.com
  One&Only Royal Mirage   04 399 9999   www oneandonlyroyalmirage.com
  Sheraton Jumeira
  Beach Resort & Towers   04 399 5533   www.starwoodhotels.com
  The Ritz-Carlton Dubai   04 399 4000   www.ritzcarlton.com

★★★★

Oasis Beach Hotel   04 399 4444   www.jebelali-international.com

Ras Al Khaimah

★★★★★

Al Hamra Fort Hotel   07 244 6666   www.alhamrafort.com
Hilton Ras Al Khaimah   07 228 8888   www.hilton.com
Khatt Springs Hotel & Spa   07 244 8777   gmoffice@khatthotel.com
Ras Al Khaimah Hotel   07 236 2999

Budget

Bin Majid Beach Resort   07 244 6644   resort@binmajid.com

Ruwais

★★★★★

Dhafra Beach Hotel   02 877 1600   www.ncityh.com

Sharjah

★★★★★

Holiday International Hotel   06 573 6666   www.holidayinternational.com
Radisson SAS Resort   06 565 7777   info.sharjah@radisson.sah.com

★★★★

Coral Beach Resort   06 522 9999   www.coral-beachresortsharjah.com
Lou Lou'a Beach Resort   06 528 5000   www.loulouabeach.com
Sharjah Grand Hotel   06 528 5557   www.sharjahgrand.com

Umm Al Quwain

Budget

Barracuda Beach Resort	06 768 1555	baracuda@eim.ae
Flamingo Beach Resort	06 765 1185	info@flamingoresort.ae

East Coast

Al Aqqa

★★★★★

● Le Meridien Al Aqah Beach Resort	09 244 9000	www.lemeridien-alaqah.com
Fujairah Rotana Resort & Spa	(Opens Jan 07)	www.rotana.com
Hotel JAL Fujairah Resort & Spa	(Opens Dec 06)	www.jalhotels.com

★★★★

Fujairah Beach Motel	09 228 111	fbm@eim.ae
● Royal Beach Al Faqeet Hotel & Resort	09 244 9444	royalbch@eim.ae

Budget

● Sandy Beach Hotel & Resort ▶ p.132	09 244 5555	www.sandybm.com

Dibba

Budget

● Holiday Beach Hotel	09 244 5540	holybemo@eim.ae

Fujairah

★★★★★

● Hilton Fujairah Resort	09 222 2411	www.hilton.com

Khor Fakkan

★★★★

Oceanic Hotel	09 238 5111	www.oceanichotel.com

Musandam

Khasab

★★★★

● Golden Tulip Resort Khasab	+968 2673 0777	www.goldentulipkhasab.com

★★★

Khasab Hotel	+968 2673 0271

Basic Arabic

Basic

Yes	na'am
No	la
Please	min fadlak (m)
	min fadliki (f)
Thank you	shukran
Please in offering	tafaddal (m)
	tafaddali (f)
Praise be to God	al-hamdu l-illah
God willing	in shaa'a l-laah

Greeting

(peace be upon you)	as-salaamu alaykom
Greeting in reply	wa alaykom is-salaam
Good morning	sabah il-khayr
Good morning in reply	sabah in-nuwr
Good evening	masa il-khayr
Good evening in reply	masa in-nuwr
Hello	marhaba
Hello in reply	marhabtayn
How are you?	kayf haalak (m)
	kayf haalik (f)
Fine, thank you	zayn, shukran (m)/zayna, shukran (f)
Welcome	ahlan wa sahlan
Welcome in reply	ahlan fiyk (m)
	ahlan fiyki (f)
Goodbye	ma is-salaama

Introduction

My name is	ismiy...
What is your name?	shuw ismak (m)
	shuw ismik (f)
Where are you from?	min wayn inta (m)/min wayn inti (f)
I am from...	anaa min...
Britain	braitani
Europe	oropi
India	al hindi
America	ameriki

Route Related

Is this the road to...	hadaa al tariyq ila
Right	yamiyn
Left	yassar
Straight ahead	siydaa
North	shamaal
South	januwb
East	sharq
West	garb

Turning	mafraq
First	awwal
Second	thaaniy
Road	tariyq
Street	shaaria'
Roundabout	duwwaar
Signals	ishaara
Close to	qarib min
Petrol station	mahattat betrol
Sea/beach	il bahar
Mountain/s	jabal/jibaal
Desert	al sahraa
Airport	mataar
Hotel	funduq
Restaurant	mata'am

Accidents

Police	al shurtaa
Permit/licence	rukhsaa
Accident	Haadith
Papers	waraq
Insurance	ta'miyn
Sorry	aasif (m)
	aasifa (f)

Questions

How many/much?	kam?
Where?	wayn?
When?	mata?
Which?	ayy?
How?	kayf?
What?	shuw?
Why?	laysh?
Who?	miyn?
To/for	ila
In/at	fee
From	min
And	wa
Also	kamaan
There isn't	maa fee

Numbers

Zero	sifr
One	waahad
Two	ithnayn
Three	thalatha
Four	arba'a
Five	khamsa
Six	sitta
Seven	saba'a
Eight	thamaanya
Nine	tiss'a
Ten	ashara
Hundred	miya
Thousand	alf

Residents' Guides
All you need to know about living, working and enjoying

Abu Dhabi · Bahrain · Dubai · Geneva · Hong Kong · Kuwait

London · New York · Oman · Qatar · Singapore · Sydney

Activity Guides
Drive, trek, dive and swim... Life will never be boring again

off-road UAE · off-road · trekking Oman · underwater UAE

Practical Guides
You've got questions, these books have answers

Dubai red-tape · Dubai starter kit · Dubai & Abu Dhabi family

Lifestyle Products
The perfect accessories
for a buzzing lifestyle

POSH NOSH — DUBAI

Mini Guides
The perfect pocket-sized
Visitors' Guides

Abu Dhabi · Dubai · Oman · Singapore · Hong Kong

Middle East · Star Restaurants · Star Bars

Maps
Wherever you are, never get lost again

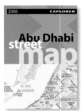  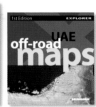 

Photography Books
Beautiful cities caught through the lens

Calendars
The time, the place,
and the date

Index

The Underwater Team

Lead Editor Tim Binks
Editor Jeanne Davies
Senior Designer Alex Jeffries
Designer Rafi Pullat
Sales Alena Palmer

Publisher Alistair MacKenzie

Editorial

Managing Editor Claire England
Editors David Quinn, Jane Roberts, Matt Farquharson,
Sean Kearns, Tim Binks
Deputy Editors Becky Lucas, Jeanne Davies
Sub Editor Jo Holden-Macdonald
Editorial Assistants Helga Becker, Mimi Stankova,
Wenda Oosterbroek

Design

Creative Director Pete Maloney
Art Director Ieyad Charaf
Senior Designer Alex Jeffries
Lead Designer Jayde Fernandes
Designers Noushad Madathil, Noushad Pathiyatt, Rafi Pullat
Cartographer Zainudheen Madathil
Design Admin Manager Shyrell Tamayo

Photography

Photography Manager Pamela Grist

Sales and Marketing

Sales Manager Alena Palmer
Sales Executive Laura Zuffa
International Sales Manager Ivan Rodrigues
Business Development Shine Ebrahim
Merchandisers Abdul Gafoor, Ahmed Mainodin,
Firos Khan, Mannie Lugtu

Finance and Administration

Administration Manager Andrea Fust
Accounts Assistant Cherry Enriquez
Administrator Enrico Maullon
Driver Rafi Jamal
Accountant A.S. Senthil Kumar

IT

IT Administrator Ajay Krishnan R.
Senior IT Engineer Smitha Sadanand
Software Engineer Tissy Varghese

Contact Us

Reader Response

If you have any comments and suggestions, fill out our online reader response form and you could win prizes.
Log on to **www.Explorer-Publishing.com**

General Enquiries

We'd love to hear your thoughts and answer any questions you have about this book or any other Explorer product.
Contact us at **Info@Explorer-Publishing.com**

Careers

If you fancy yourself as an Explorer, send your CV (stating the position you're interested in) to **Jobs@Explorer-Publishing.com**

Designlab and Contract Publishing

For enquiries about Explorer's Contract Publishing arm and design services contact **Designlab@Explorer-Publishing.com**

Maps

For cartography enquiries, including orders and comments, contact **Maps@Explorer-Publishing.com**

Corporate Sales

For bulk sales and customisation options, for this book or any Explorer product, contact **Sales@Explorer-Publishing.com**

Explorer Publishing & Distribution
Office 51B, Zomorrodah Building, Za'abeel Road
PO Box 34275, Dubai, United Arab Emirates
Phone: +971 (0)4 335 3520, **Fax:** +971 (0)4 335 3529
Info@Explorer-Publishing.com
www.Explorer-Publishing.com

Notes

Please take the time to visit our website (www.Explorer-Publishing.com) and pass along your comments, notes, thoughts and corrections on any aspect (directions, maps, text, photographs, routes) of this book. Your feedback is essential for us to improve our guidebooks.

Happy exploring!

Map Sketch

Explorer Publishing & Distribution, Office 51B, Zomorrodah Building, Za'abeel Road PO Box 34275, Dubai, United Arab Emirates **Phone** (+971 4) 335 3520 **Fax** (+971 4) 335 3529 **Email** Info@Explorer-Publishing.com www.Explorer-Publishing.com

Notes

Map Sketch

Explorer Publishing & Distribution, Office 51B, Zomorrodah Building, Za'abeel Road
PO Box 34275, Dubai, United Arab Emirates **Phone** (+971 4) 335 3520 **Fax** (+971 4) 335 3529
Email Info@Explorer-Publishing.com www.Explorer-Publishing.com